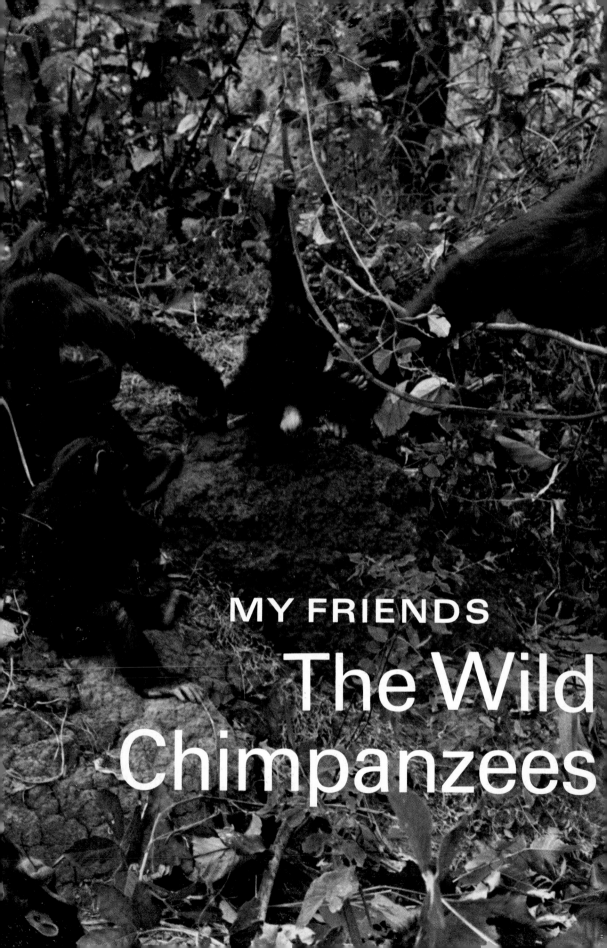

MY FRIENDS
The Wild
Chimpanzees

BY BARONESS JANE VAN LAWICK-GOODALL

PHOTOGRAPHS BY BARON HUGO VAN LAWICK

FOREWORD BY LEONARD CARMICHAEL
Vice President for Research and Exploration
National Geographic Society

PREPARED BY NATIONAL GEOGRAPHIC
SPECIAL PUBLICATIONS DIVISION
Robert L. Breeden, Chief

NATIONAL GEOGRAPHIC SOCIETY
Melville Bell Grosvenor, President and Editor
WASHINGTON, D.C.

My Friends
The Wild Chimpanzees
by Baroness Jane van Lawick-Goodall
Photographs by Baron Hugo van Lawick

Published by
The National Geographic Society
Melville Bell Grosvenor, *President and Editor*

Foreword by
Leonard Carmichael,
Vice President for Research and Exploration

Gilbert M. Grosvenor, *Editorial Director*

The fourth in a series of National
Geographic Books from the Special
Publications Division.

Robert L. Breeden, *Editor*
Donald J. Crump, *Associate Editor*
Philip B. Silcott, *Manuscript Editor*
Theodore S. Amussen, *Assistant to the
    Editor and Liaison with the Author*
Andrew H. Brown, *Editorial Consultant*
Cynthia R. Ramsay, *Research*
Mary Ann Harrell, *Research and Style*
David R. Bridge, *Picture Editor*
Joseph A. Taney, *Art Director*
Josephine B. Bolt, *Assistant Art Director*
Ronald M. Fisher, *Production*
James R. Whitney, *Engraving and Printing*
Picture Legends: Theodore S. Amussen,
    David R. Bridge, Ronald M. Fisher,
    Mary Ann Harrell, Gerald S. Snyder
Editorial Assistants: Luba Balko, Margaret
    S. Dean

Austin Briggs, *paintings and drawings,
    Chapter I, and painting, pages 88-89*
Richard Schlecht, *painting, pages 46-47*
Jay H. Matternes, *all other paintings
    and drawings*

*Alone in ape country, Baroness Jane
van Lawick-Goodall takes to the trees
to see above grass that grows as high
as 14 feet. Overleaf: The young
British scientist moves freely among
the chimps. Sustained observation
enabled her to recognize many on
sight and give them names.*

Foreword

This astonishingly novel and interesting book means a great deal to me. I am one of the few fortunate outsiders to have had the privilege of visiting Baroness Jane van Lawick-Goodall at her field station when she was in the midst of the epoch-making studies of wild chimpanzees that she reports here. I have myself for more than a quarter of a century had quite close contact with scientific studies of live chimpanzees in laboratory colonies in America. But when I saw at close range thirty or more of these magnificent animals in their native forests bordering Africa's Lake Tanganyika, my eyes were opened wide to a wholly new and scientifically important understanding of chimpanzee behavior in the wild.

Because of their highly evolved bodies and brains, chimpanzees along with gorillas and orangutans—the so-called Great Apes—have been intensively studied since 1913, when Wolfgang Köhler began his pioneer research on the intelligence of chimpanzees. Recently the United States Government wisely provided funds for the establishment of seven primate research centers in association with American medical schools to further the study of these animals. One practical application of such work has been the effective use of chimpanzee subjects in developing the equipment necessary for safe human space travel.

But in spite of these long and fruitful years of laboratory research and of some good preliminary natural-habitat observations by such scientists as Henry W. Nissen, no one had concentrated on the full cycle—year after year—of the life-maintaining activities of a defined wild population of these great animals until the author undertook her insightful study of chimpanzees in 1960.

The unique and vital photographs in the book were selected from many thousands made by the author's talented husband, photographer Baron Hugo van Lawick. The beautiful and zoologically accurate paintings and drawings of artist Jay Matternes present with uncanny realism many of the activities of these powerful and sometimes violent primates.

Thus this book adds a new and significant dimension to man's knowledge of the chimpanzee—the Great Ape that is in so many ways more like man than any other living animal.

Leonard Carmichael

Vice President for Research and Exploration
National Geographic Society

Contents

*"Majestic and dignified in their freedom," the author
says of the wild chimpanzees she has come to know so well.*

1

An Old Dream, a New Life

HIGH ABOVE OUR HEADS four wild chimpanzees busily gathered their last meal of the day, moving from branch to branch in a large fig tree as they deftly plucked the ripe fruit with their lips. Patches of golden light danced on their black coats as the late-afternoon sun filtered through the leaves.

My husband Hugo and I sat in silence, content to watch. We had been away for a year, and it was wonderful to be back, deep in the forest of Tanzania's Gombe Stream Game Reserve, and far from the bustle of civilization. We recognized the chimpanzees overhead as old acquaintances, and they showed by their calm acceptance of our presence that they remembered us. Had we been strangers they would have fled, just as six years earlier all the chimps had run from me.

With the approach of evening, the tropical sun sank swiftly, and we shivered as its warmth left the forest. One by one the chimpanzees stopped collecting fruit and sat gazing out over the trees as they chewed their last mouthfuls.

Finally, old Mr. Worzle climbed down slowly and hobbled to another tree. Pulling himself into the foliage, he began building a bed. The nomadic chimps make a new sleeping platform every evening, selecting a tree wherever dusk finds them.

Choosing a broad, horizontally forked bough, Mr. Worzle bent the surrounding limbs down over it, holding each in place with his feet. Although his hands are stiff and gnarled, as if crippled with arthritis, he easily snapped with one hand branches a man would find hard to break with two. After five minutes, he stood on a springy, leafy mattress. He lay down, but seemed uncomfortable, for he kept changing

Approaching the beach of Gombe Stream Game Reserve, the author
scans the hills where she will begin her study of wild chimpanzees.

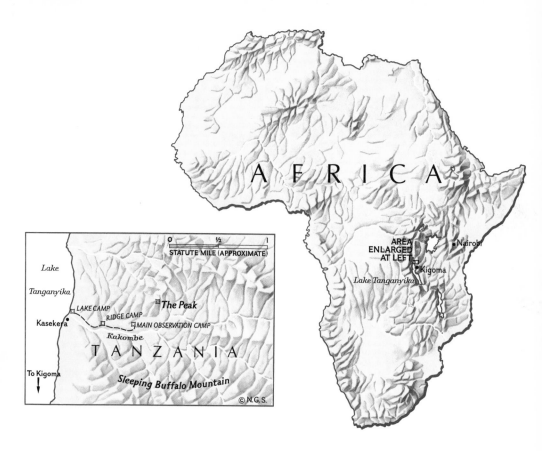

AFRICA

AREA ENLARGED AT LEFT

Nairobi

Kigoma

Lake Tanganyika

© N.G.S.

0   ½   1
STATUTE MILE (APPROXIMATE)

Lake

Tanganyika

LAKE CAMP

☐ The Peak

RIDGE CAMP

Kasekera

☐ MAIN OBSERVATION CAMP

Kakombe

T A N Z A N I A

To Kigoma

Sleeping Buffalo Mountain

Mountain laboratory for the study of chimpanzees in their natural habitat, Gombe Stream Game Reserve lies near the heart of Africa. The sanctuary, accessible only by boat, harbors more than 100 of the Great Apes.

his position. Finally he sat up, reached out to pick several leafy twigs, placed them under his head, and, satisfied at last, settled down for the night.

Hugo and I gazed up at the three remaining apes— Pepe, a magnificent young male about twelve years old, his seven-year-old sister Miff, and their tiny brother Merlin. Miff, after tilting her head and looking about, swung from the fig tree and began building a nest at the top of a palm. Merlin followed at once and sat close by, watching as she worked.

For the first time, we saw Merlin clearly. His appearance shocked us. "He looks like a starving child," I whispered to Hugo. "It's amazing that he's still alive."

Merlin's aged mother had died a year before, and his sister Miff had adopted him. But Miff had not been able to provide the security of a mother, nor the milk a wild chimp needs until he is at least three. As we stared at the wizened midget with his huge, apathetic eyes, his matchstick arms and legs, and his swollen belly, we found it difficult to believe he was the same chimp we had known as a healthy two-year-old.

"Can he really be three?" whispered Hugo. "He doesn't seem to have grown at all in the last year, does he?" I agreed. If anything, he seemed smaller.

Her nest completed, Miff lay down. A moment longer Merlin sat, so tiny he was barely discernible in the gathering dusk; then he crept into the large bed and curled up close beside his sister for the night. Pepe, meanwhile, had made a nest nearby. Everything grew quiet.

Reluctantly, Hugo and I left them and started back along the animal track toward Ridge Camp, where we relax at day's end. At one point we had to cross a narrow, cascading mountain stream; at another, crawl beneath a thorny tangle of branches and lianas that overhung the trail. Then, after pushing through a stretch of head-high grass, we reached the track leading to our little dining hut.

The grass-roofed, three-walled structure stands on a ridge offering a view as beautiful and peaceful as any I have ever seen. To the west lies the shining expanse of Lake Tanganyika, one of the largest and deepest freshwater lakes in the world. Above the ridge, green mountains climb the eastern sky, their deep ravines thick with forests and laced by murmuring streams.

As we approached the hut that evening, the last flush of a blood-red sunset lingered above a dark ribbon of mountains on the far side of the lake. Overhead, fronds of graceful oil palms swayed against the glowing sky.

At Ridge Camp our assistants awaited us, Caroline Coleman, a graduate student of zoology from Bristol University, and Sally Avery, who had formerly helped operate two dairy farms in Kenya. They had replaced Edna Koning and Sonia Ivey, our first helpers at the reserve. Two visitors also greeted us: Michael Fisher, Hugo's half brother, at the reserve to make drawings of insects, and young John MacKinnon, who had come from England to study insect behavior before beginning the fall term at Oxford University.

After joining them, we sat outside the tent, listening to the symphony of the African night: the whispering of trees, the chirping of crickets, the distant sighing of water on the beach, an occasional rustling in the grass as some small creature scurried past.

The sky had become quite dark when Anyango, the camp cook, served supper—a delicious fish stew that is a specialty of the Gombe Stream Reserve. *"Habari ya kazi?"*— "How is the work?"—he asked as he laid out the food. We told him of sighting four old friends and of the poor condition of

little Merlin. Shaking his head in sympathy, he walked back toward the African camp on the beach.

"Oh, we mustn't forget the genet," Michael said as he put fish on a saucer and placed it on the ground near the tent. About 20 minutes later, we saw the small nocturnal creature peering at us from behind a clump of grass, her whiskers twitching. Hugo and I had first noticed the genet more than a year before as she prowled past on nightly hunts. We had put out food and gradually she had come to expect the extra meal. Caroline and Sally had continued feeding her while we were away from the reserve.

Now we saw her long, pointed face, daintily marked with black and gray. Unafraid, she crouched over the helping of fish. The lamplight picked out the black broken stripes running the length of her narrow gray body, and the black bands around her long tail. The meal finished, she washed her face with her paws—rubbing cheeks, whiskers, and behind each round ear. Then she vanished silently into the night.

Soon after, we left John and Michael, who were staying at Ridge Camp, and set off in the darkness for the main chimpanzee observation camp about a mile up the Kakombe Stream valley. The four of us walked single file along the narrow trail, which presently wound through a patch of thick forest

Extra guest for supper, a nocturnal genet eats fish from a saucer. The small carnivore learned to expect the free meal after Jane and her husband, Baron Hugo van Lawick, noticed it prowling past, and began putting out food.

where the foliage arched overhead and blotted out the stars.

Indicating a bend in the track with his flashlight, Hugo told Caroline and Sally that once we had found a dead bushbuck there. "We thought it was a leopard's kill," he said, "and late at night we crept back to see if he had returned for another feed."

The episode remained vivid in my memory: As Hugo and I were moving silently toward the spot, we heard the crunching of bone only yards away in the blackness. Hastily we retreated, and from a safer distance aimed a flashlight in the direction of the sound. Two red eyes glared at us in the light.

"Our knees felt a bit weak until we realized it was only a bushpig," Hugo continued. "But he did look huge and gruesome, with a piece of half-eaten leg sticking out of his mouth."

"It's not surprising that we thought a leopard had made the kill," I said. "We knew there were at least two of them living in this valley."

Topping one last steep slope, we saw a glow of light from two metal buildings nestled against the mountainside. Buildings! It was still hard for Hugo and me to believe that they really existed. They had stood there for a year before we had a chance to move in. No sooner were they finished in March, 1965, than we had to leave, I to complete my last two terms of residence at Cambridge University and prepare the thesis for my doctorate in animal behavior, and Hugo to edit a chimpanzee film for the National Geographic Society.

When we reached the Main Observation Camp, Hugo and I walked to our house, leaving Caroline and Sally to go to their rooms in the larger building where we transcribe notes and analyze and file the results of our research.

As I was dropping off to sleep I heard a chimpanzee calling. The long, drawn out, rather melancholy hoots rose high above the dark trees of the valley.

"I wonder if that's Mr. Worzle having a nightmare?" I asked, and Hugo laughed drowsily.

The calls stopped, but I did not go to sleep at once. I lay listening to the murmur of the stream in the valley below, and watching through the open door the silhouette of a feathery acacia tree.

"How different everything is," I thought. "When I started here six years ago, it seemed the chimpanzees would never let me come near them. I was largely inexperienced, and alone save for my mother and an African cook. Today the chimpanzees accept me, I have my Ph.D. degree, two European helpers, a staff of six Africans, and — most important of all — my husband Hugo!" Certainly life had changed since I first began studying *Pan satyrus schweinfurthi,* the eastern or long-haired chimpanzee found in the Gombe Stream Reserve.

My love for animals began early. As a child, I saved my pocket money to buy secondhand books on animals, and spent most of my free time writing descriptions of the habits of the animals and birds around home in Bournemouth, England.

I left school at 18 and worked as a secretary, first in Oxford and later in London, all the while looking forward to the day when I could go to Africa to study animals in the wild. Where else could I find such an abundance, such a variety, of fascinating creatures?

After saving enough to pay the fare, I arrived in Nairobi, Kenya, in 1957. The thrill of that day remains vivid in my memory. I had taken a big step toward realizing my dream. Just one month later I met Dr. Louis S. B. Leakey, famed anthropologist and paleontologist, to whom I confided my life-long ambition. He suggested that I start work at the Coryndon (now National) Museum of Natural History in Nairobi, where I served as his secretary.

Later, I accompanied Dr. Leakey and his wife Mary on one of their digs at Olduvai Gorge, which reaches a depth of 300 feet in places as it cuts through the dry, windswept Serengeti Plain. The thorn scrub and acacia trees, the brittle, yellow grass, the glowing flame color of the aloes and the cruel spikes of the sansevieria, a wild bowstring hemp, all epitomized the Africa I had read about for so long.

Every day we worked from dawn until nearly dusk, picking with small knives and dental probes at the crumbling rock surface, gently removing the fossilized remains of creatures that roamed the African countryside more than a million years ago. In the evenings I explored the surrounding plains. I saw, as I wandered about on foot and unarmed, the lion and the rhinoceros, the dik-dik and the giraffe.

I THINK that during those weeks at Olduvai Dr. Leakey realized my interest in animals was not merely a passing one. Not long after we returned to Nairobi he suggested that I study the behavior of chimpanzees in the wild.

"You see," said Dr. Leakey, "although the chimpanzee has been known to science for nearly three centuries, and although, because of the ape's similarity to man, it has been used extensively as an experimental animal in medicine and in space-related research, only one real attempt has been made to study chimps in their natural habitat. That was by Dr. Henry Nissen in French Guinea about 30 years ago, and he stayed in the field only two and a half months.

"There are all sorts of reasons," Dr. Leakey went on, "why it's important that someone make a careful study of chimps in the wild. For one thing, it may soon be too late. Man is rapidly penetrating and cultivating new areas, killing the animals and destroying their habitats.

"For another thing, details about the behavior of one of the most manlike creatures living today, in its natural state, may give us useful pointers as to the habits of prehistoric man himself."

Of course I was wildly enthusiastic; but 18 months passed before Dr. Leakey could get funds for me: a grant from the Wilkie Foundation in Illinois, an organization which supports studies of man and the other primates. The money would provide for a preliminary investigation of chimpanzees at the Gombe Stream Reserve.

In June, 1960, I left Nairobi by Land-Rover on the 840-mile journey to Kigoma, the point of civilization nearest the reserve. My mother accompanied me, eagerly volunteering when she heard that the authorities refused to allow me to live alone in the bush.

We found Kigoma a small but fairly busy town of roughly 14,000 inhabitants. Some 770 miles of railway link it with Dar es Salaam, capital of Tanzania, and its lake harbor provides dockage for vessels plying to and from Burundi, Zambia, and the Democratic Republic of the Congo.

My mother and I strolled the main part of the town near the lake shore, around the *boma*, or administrative center. There we found the post office and the police station as well as a bank and a hotel. From this central area an asphalt road, bordered by mango trees, follows a dead straight, slightly up-hill course for about a mile. Then it curves and changes into a red-earth highway—the only main road leading out of Kigoma. Rows of *dukas*, the small stores where we purchased some of our supplies, flank the road.

During our walks, we saw a hospital, several schools, and a gay and bustling outdoor market. We stayed in Kigoma only long enough to order a month's provisions and search for a cook to accompany us.

Finally we had everything ready. The Game Ranger for the area, David Anstey, had arranged one of his semi-annual visits to the reserve to coincide with our arrival, and we rode with him in the government launch, towing our own 12-foot dinghy with its tiny outboard motor. The little boat would provide us our only link with the civilized world. With us came Dominic, the African cook we had employed.

As we chugged slowly along the shoreline I gazed at the mountains rising steeply from the lake, and my mind seethed with questions—questions that only time would answer. How easily would I be able to find my way around the rugged country? How long would it take the chimpanzees to get used to me? Would it be easy to find them? But more than any other feeling, excitement welled up within me as I tried to guess what lay ahead.

Shortly after noon, we arrived at Kasekera, a point about midway along the ten-mile coastline of the small reserve. On the beach, under the shade of huge mango trees, stood

Bushpig crunching on the remains of an antelope startles the young scientist and her photographer husband. Hearing the snap of bone in the darkness, the couple believed they had approached a leopard feeding on its kill.

the huts of two Game Scouts who patrol the shores of the reserve. Nearby lived an honorary headman, Iddi Matata, and his family, who had permission to stay on the reserve as company for the scouts and their wives. Several ramshackle temporary fishing huts dotted the shore.

With introductions and greetings completed, David Anstey led us up from the beach and along an animal trail to a small clearing shaded by three tall palms and close to a cool mountain stream.

"I suggest that, for a while anyway, you put your tent here," he said. "The scouts are almost within earshot, and they'll be able to help you if you need them during your first few weeks."

The spot delighted us. With the help of David and the two scouts, we quickly pitched our tent. Then I hurried away to explore. The long grass that covers the more open slopes had burned off during a recent fire, leaving the surface of the mountainside loose and treacherous. The sun beat down, its heat dry and intense. As I climbed higher I could see the lake—flat as a mirror and dazzling with reflected sunlight.

I found no chimpanzees, only a troop of about 50

baboons moving slowly across the ground picking insects and seeds from the charred grass. When they saw me, the youngsters barked frenziedly and slapped at the ground or shook twigs with quick, jerky movements of their hands. The adult males, less demonstrative, occasionally gave loud alarm barks or bared great, curved dog teeth in a wide yawn called the canine display. Finally the troop, disturbed by my intrusion, moved over a ridge and out of sight.

As I returned to camp, my clothes a mess from sliding down one of the fire-blackened slopes, I was well aware of some of the many difficulties facing me. Equally, I knew the day was one of the happiest of my life. That night, after supper around a campfire, I pulled my low bed out beneath the palm trees and slept under the stars.

At first everything was new and exciting. It did not matter too much that the chimpanzees fled when they saw me in the distance. They would get used to me. And when I almost slipped in a vain attempt to climb a more or less unscalable precipice, or got myself hopelessly entangled trying to push through more or less impenetrable undergrowth—well, I would know better next time.

I recall vividly my first encounter with a bull buffalo on one of those trails. He had been dozing in the tall grass, and I almost bumped into him. Luckily the wind was in my favor, and I made a wide detour to prevent his picking up my scent. Lone buffaloes do not frequent the reserve, and I have wondered if he was the same one that treed an African fisherman down near the beach. I had seen the tree, its trunk gashed innumerable times by the enraged animal's horns.

On another occasion a leopard passed within a few yards of me before it turned and bounded into the undergrowth. When walking along the lake shore, I sometimes saw the one resident hippo, submerged with only his eyes, ears, and nostrils visible. Once, as I waded around a rocky headland, a Storm's water cobra, carried by a wave, brushed my foot. I stood stock still until the water carried it away. There is no serum for the venom of this deadly snake—a species found only in Lake Tanganyika.

But as the weeks passed, the chimpanzees continued to flee and I often despaired. Of course I saw chimps, but seldom got near enough to learn anything really worthwhile. Mostly I saw them in the distance, feeding in trees; if I attempted to approach closer than 500 yards they fled. Sometimes I tramped all day through the mountains, from valley to valley, and only heard chimpanzees calling from afar.

Whenever I found a group feeding in a tree ripe with fruit, I made a small blind nearby after the chimps had left, hoping they would return the following day. But if they did, they almost always spotted me crouched behind my tangle of branches and, after staring intently, dropped to the ground and disappeared.

Even when they failed to detect me, there were usually other snags—either the dense foliage of the valleys obscured most of their activities, or else a troop of baboons passed by. The baboons, with their incredibly acute eyesight, never failed to see me, however well I concealed myself. Their loud barks of alarm quickly drew the chimpanzees' attention to the fact that something was amiss, and the shy apes stopped feeding at once and vanished.

After such experiences I often returned to camp in utter discouragement. Was my whole attempt doomed to failure? At such times my mother boosted my morale. She would relate the events of her own day, telling me about the plants and insects that she was collecting because she wanted to do something useful while at the reserve. I must have been a trying companion at times, but she helped to keep me smiling, and for that I shall always be grateful.

Two MONTHS after our arrival, my mother and I were laid low by some fever—almost certainly a type of malaria. We had been told that there were no malarial mosquitoes in the area, and were naive enough then to believe it. So we had no proper drugs with us.

For ten days we lay side by side in our hot, airless tent, almost too weak to move. We had just energy enough to pick up the thermometer from time to time and read our temperatures—my mother's remained above 105° for five days, falling slightly only during the cooler nights. After our recovery, we looked back over that ordeal and realized how close she had come to death.

While we lay ill, Dominic showed touching concern and thoughtfulness. With his own money he bought eggs to try to tempt our appetites with light custards and fluffy omelets. We found, too, that he kept watch over us during the night. Once

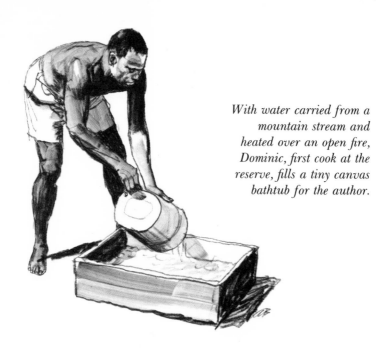

With water carried from a mountain stream and heated over an open fire, Dominic, first cook at the reserve, fills a tiny canvas bathtub for the author.

my mother wandered out in near delirium and collapsed unconscious beside a palm tree. I was delirious myself and quite unaware that she had left the tent. Dominic found her there in the small hours of the morning and carried her back to her bed. He begged us to go into Kigoma to see a doctor, but the very thought of a three-hour trip in our little open boat was enough to make our temperatures shoot up. So we just lay there, occasionally eating a dry biscuit or a dish of soup, until the fevers spent themselves.

As it happened, the illness marked the turning point in my efforts to get better acquainted with the chimpanzees. On my first morning back in the field, I still suffered from weakness and dizziness. Sweating and exhausted, my head pounding and my heart hammering against my ribs, I reached a rocky peak some 1,000 feet above lake level. As I sat there to recover my wind I heard chimpanzees calling. Just below me, a large group was feeding in a patch of fig trees, stuffing themselves with fruit.

My recovery had coincided with the start of the four-week wild-fig season in our valley. Day after day I returned to what I called the Peak, and each time I saw chimps. One of their paths crossed the ridge below and another traversed the slopes above. Because I always stationed myself in the same place and never crept up to them or appeared unexpectedly, the chimps at last began to accept me. I started filling in details of their way of life—their feeding behavior, the ever-changing composition of the small groups that make up their community, and their habit of making new nests each night.

Toward the end of the fig season I began cautiously moving down from the Peak and approaching the apes more closely. They often ran away, but there were wonderful moments when they let me sit near enough to watch them without binoculars. I began to recognize some of them as individuals and gave them names that seemed to suit them. They are as distinct, one from another, as human beings. Mr. McGregor stood out from the others because of his bald crown and shoulders—the result apparently of some kind of skin disorder, since I have never seen another chimp as bald as he. For some reason he reminded me of the crusty old gardener in the Peter Rabbit books.

Then there was Flo, with her unbelievably ugly face, her torn and ragged ears. She had an infant daughter, Fifi, and two sons, Figan and Faben, then about four and eight years of age respectively. Mr. Worzle was startling in his appearance: His eyes resemble those of a man. That part of the eye around the iris is white, instead of being heavily pigmented with brown as in other chimps.

Handsome David Greybeard—with his white beard and his calm, gentle disposition—was the first to allow me to approach closely without running away. His quick-tempered, powerfully built companion, Goliath, held the top rank in the community when I named him. Mike, another handsome male, was destined to bluff Goliath from his top social position. Mike's excitable, aggressive friend J. B. got his name because of his resemblance (in my mind) to John Bull—the stout figure that typifies the aggressive, pugnacious Englishman. His tough masculine character has since earned him the nickname "007," after the hero of Ian Fleming's novels.

I became acquainted with Huxley, a tall slender male with a distinguished and slightly professional air, and named him for Sir Julian Huxley, the biologist, and with the well-built, rugged Leakey—named, of course, for Dr. Leakey himself. Eventually I came to know some 50 chimps. But at least 60 others that live in the reserve have never ventured into the camp where we now feed the chimps on a regular basis.

The 15 square miles of rugged country where I did most of my work soon seemed as familiar as though I had roamed them all my life. My sense of balance adjusted to the steep, slippery surfaces, and my skin toughened against the scratching and tearing of the knife-edged sword grass and the dense undergrowth. The animal trails, used alike by buffalo and bushbuck, chimp and baboon, became almost as easy for me to travel as the lanes and byways of the English countryside.

M Y MOTHER returned to England after a five-month stay, but by then I had the approval of the authorities to remain at the reserve. I missed her, for she had been a staunch companion, never complaining of the rough conditions or the narrow camp bed that sometimes pitched her onto the ground when she tossed at night. She had not been afraid when I slept in the mountains, leaving her alone in camp. Without her I would have had difficulty in keeping my chin up during those long weeks of discouragement.

For ten months I remained at the reserve without European company, but my endless work kept me from being lonely. Every day I arose no later than 5:30 so I could move close to the chimps before first light. Frequently my elusive subjects slipped away within an hour. At other times I spent most of the day near the chimps, filling half a notebook with observations. I recorded everything I saw, no matter how insignificant it seemed.

Later, when I analyzed my notes, I found that much which seemed trivial when I jotted it down had since acquired significance. For example, when a chimpanzee scratches himself during a grooming session the action does not necessarily imply that he has an itch. Often it serves to indicate that part of his body he wants his companion to groom.

On my return to camp in the evenings I bathed in a small canvas tub, had supper by the campfire, then transcribed the day's notes by the light of two hurricane lamps. The task sometimes lasted until long past midnight, and there would be ten to fifteen pages of longhand to add to my files.

During these months, Dominic's wife and little daughter joined us, and from Kenya came Hassan, Dr. Leakey's boatman for more than a decade. He took over our small craft and began making the monthly shopping trips to Kigoma. I no longer had to leave the reserve even for a day. Nor did I worry about finances, for I had received a letter advising me that I could continue my project under a grant from the National Geographic Society's Committee for Research and Exploration. Now I could devote all my time and energy to the chimpanzees I had come so far to study.

*First tent at the reserve goes up with the help
of a Ranger and two Game Scouts. Although
aware that many difficulties lay ahead, Jane recalls
the day as "one of the happiest of my life."*

Dying embers and a cup of coffee dispel the chill of an African night at the author's first camp. Frustration, even despair, marked her early days on the reserve. "There were times," she says, "when I wondered if the chimps would ever permit me to approach them." At left, she struggles with a balky outboard on Lake Tanganyika, her only route to civilization. In a cool mountain stream she lathers her blonde hair.

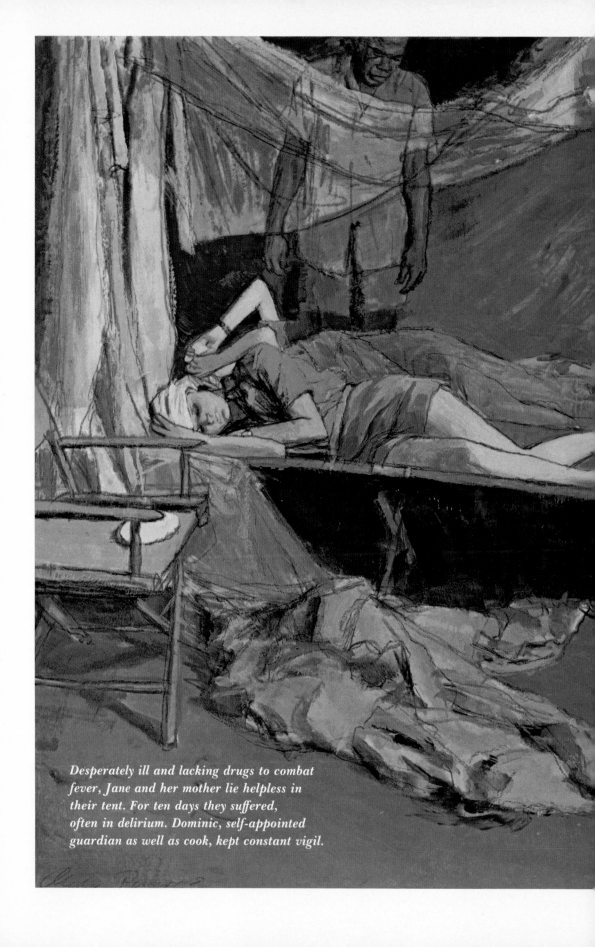

Desperately ill and lacking drugs to combat
fever, Jane and her mother lie helpless in
their tent. For ten days they suffered,
often in delirium. Dominic, self-appointed
guardian as well as cook, kept constant vigil.

Ripping a hole in a roof—and in a theory—determined David Greybeard steals a stem of bananas from a new storeroom, presumably chimp-proof.

2

At Long Last I Belong

AT THE START of the rainy season in 1960, after four long, difficult months in the field, I made my first really exciting observation—I saw a chimp fashion and use crude tools!

That morning I felt rather despondent, for I had trudged the mountains for hours and had seen no chimpanzees at all. Then, as I headed for the Peak, I spotted a black shape beside the red-earth mound of a termite nest.

Quickly I sat down (even today the chimps seem more at ease if we observe them from their own level) and peered through my binoculars. I saw David Greybeard, and as I watched him I could hardly believe my eyes. He was carefully trimming the edges from a wide blade of sword grass!

I gazed, scarcely daring to breathe, as he pushed the modified stem into the nest. He left it for a moment, then pulled it out and picked off something with his lips. The chimp continued probing with the stem until it bent double. He then discarded it and reached out to pick a length of vine. With a sweeping movement of one hand, he stripped the leaves from the vine, bit a piece from one end, and set to work again with his newly prepared tool.

For an hour I watched. From time to time David changed position, opening up new holes in the termite mound by scratching at the soil with his index finger. Finally, after again trying each of the holes in turn, he dropped the piece of vine and wandered away.

I hurried to the place and found a horde of worker termites busily sealing the holes David had opened. Each moistened bits of clay with saliva and pressed the minute pellets into place. Poking a blade of grass down one hole, I felt the insects bite it. When I pulled the stem out, four workers and a couple of the larger soldiers clung to it. I tasted one, for I make it a point to try almost everything the chimps eat, but it seemed rather flavorless to me. At that time my mother had not yet left the reserve, and I was so excited I could hardly wait for sunset to hurry down and tell her what I had seen.

"You see," I told her, "some wild animals can *use* objects as tools. There's the sea otter for one. It gets a flat stone from the floor of the sea, floats on its back with the stone lying on its chest, and bangs shellfish against it to open them. And wild chimps have been seen *using* tools. In West Africa an observer saw one poke a stick into honey in an underground bees' nest. A chimpanzee in Liberia hammered with a rock at a dried palm nut. But David didn't simply *use* tools — he actually *made* them!"

"Can you really say that he was truly making tools?" my mother asked.

I described how David had stripped leaves from the section of vine and trimmed the edges off the blade of grass.

"He didn't just make use of any old bit of material lying around," I explained. "He actually modified stems and grasses and made them suitable for his purpose."

"Then that means man isn't the only toolmaker after all!" my mother exclaimed.

ANTHROPOLOGISTS, other social scientists, and theologians have defined man in a variety of ways. Until recently one widely accepted element of the anthropologists' definition was that "man starts at that stage of primate evolution when the creature begins to make tools to a regular and set pattern." The grasses and twigs used by the chimps for termite fishing do not, perhaps, comply entirely with this specification. Nonetheless, Dr. Leakey, on learning of my findings and referring to the description above, wrote, "I feel that scientists holding to this definition are faced with three choices: They must accept chimpanzees as man, by definition; they must redefine man; or they must redefine tools."

It is of great satisfaction to me to know that my work at the Gombe Stream Game Reserve is being taken into consideration by many scientists in their continuing efforts to redefine man in a manner far more complex and detailed than ever before attempted.

As the weeks passed, I discovered that when the rains

begin the worker termites extend the passages of the nest to the surface and seal them with a thin layer of soil until it is time for the fertile, winged forms to fly out. Then the termites open the passages and the princes and princesses, as they are called, emerge and eventually join swarms from other nests. Pair by pair they burrow into the ground to form new colonies. With one batch gone, the termites again seal the passages until the next group takes wing.

Other inhabitants of the reserve also feed on termites. Baboons, monkeys, and birds gather around a nest when the emigrations take place, capturing the insects as they fly out. But the chimpanzee, using primitive tools, gets a head start while the nests are still sealed.

Many times since that first thrilling day I have watched chimpanzees fishing for termites. Usually they work about an hour. But if the insects refuse to bite, the chimps try one fishing tool after another in quick succession (as though they feel the tools are to blame), then wander away, often to try their luck at another nest.

Some authorities suggest that only when an implement is kept for future use is the toolmaker showing forethought; for this reason people often ask whether the chimps ever save the tools for reuse. This would have little point, since most of the objects would shrivel and become useless if kept. And, anyway, grass stems and twigs abound near the termite nests.

The chimpanzees do, however, select stems beforehand and carry them to termite nests quite out of sight, as far away as 100 yards. Such behavior seems to indicate a certain forethought. A mature male once picked a grass tool that he carried for half a mile while he carefully inspected eight nests. When none of them proved right for working, he gave up and dropped the stem.

The year following the discovery of chimpanzee toolmaking, I found that the apes also eat several species of ant. One, the safari ant, has a particularly vicious and painful sting. Hugo and I once saw Mr. McGregor raiding an underground nest of these insects.

Standing upright, he carefully pushed a yard-long stick into the burrow, then stepped back from the hundreds of ants that emerged. After picking off those that had bitten onto him, he returned to the nest and pulled out the stick with a magnificent gesture. Still upright, he ate the globular mass of ants clinging to the end, seemingly unmindful of the stings. Then he pushed the stick back for more.

"I'm sure early man must have used sticks and twigs as tools long before he thought of chipping flakes of stone—don't you think so?" Hugo asked.

I nodded. "In fact, Mr. McGregor looks rather like a prehistoric man himself," I said.

Indeed, the old male chimp with his bald crown, neck, and shoulders, and the little fluff of hair around his head that resembles a monk's tonsure, did look like some strange hairy man of the forest standing there, stick in hand, among the hanging lianas and gnarled trunks.

Chimps also eat weaver ants in large quantities, and we feel the apes have made quite a discovery here: The ants have a most exotic flavor, rather like curried lemon. One might even be able to market them as tropical delicacies. In addition, we have seen the chimps spend hours eating caterpillars and apparently relishing them.

I vividly recall the day deep in the forest when Hugo and I saw young Evered reach out, strip the leaves from a small branch, and stuff them into his mouth.

"Whatever is he doing?" asked Hugo as Evered took the leaves out of his mouth after chewing them slightly. Soon we had the answer. Holding them between his index and middle fingers, he dipped them into a little hollow in the trunk of a fallen tree. He lifted out the slightly mashed greenery, and we saw the gleam of water. Evered sucked the liquid from his homemade "sponge," and continued to dip and drink until he emptied the bowl.

We have seen many other chimps drink in the same way when they could not reach the water with their lips—and always, like Evered, they first chew the leaves briefly. It is the initial crumpling that makes this tool so sophisticated, for it increases the absorbency of the leaves. Here again, the Gombe Stream chimps, by modifying natural objects and using them for a specific purpose, demonstrate their ability to make tools.

Chimpanzees on some occasions use leaves for wiping themselves clean of sticky or unpleasant substances such as mud, blood, or food smears. Figan once rubbed his chest with several handfuls of leaves after carrying a load of overripe bananas. Mothers usually scrub themselves with bunches of leaves if they are dirtied by their babies. And we watched

Entranced, Jane sits motionless to avoid frightening a female bushbuck. When its nose touched her knee, the antelope bounded away in terror.

Melissa, after a fight, blotting the blood on her nose with a leaf.

"She looks like a fastidious lady dabbing at her nose-bleed with a lace hanky," Edna said. At that moment we all began to laugh, for Melissa, quite unlike a fastidious lady, licked the blood from her forest handkerchief.

There has long been discussion among some scientists as to whether man first used objects as tools or as weapons. Of course, one cannot draw firm conclusions from the Gombe Stream chimpanzee community, but these chimps do employ objects in both food-gathering and fighting. Weapon use, however, is neither as frequent nor as effective as tool use.

For instance, some adult males throw missiles with definite aim during aggressive encounters with other chimpanzees, with baboons, and with humans. Although the missiles usually travel in the right direction, they often fall short of the target and frequently are too small or ineffective to inflict damage anyway. Once Mr. Worzle threw three times in quick succession with a beautiful overarm style, scoring two hits on a big male baboon only three feet away. As weapons he used a handful of leaves, a banana skin, and a small pebble.

Only twice have we seen an adult female throw objects. But young Fifi during her sixth year gradually became a frequent, if unsuccessful, flinger of missiles, and she developed a technique all her own. Looking in any direction but that of the baboon or chimpanzee that has aroused her hostility, she unobtrusively gathers as many pebbles as she can hold. Then, with what we refer to as "Fifi's evil face," she charges toward her target and throws the whole handful. Luckily for her victims, Fifi's aim is far from good — the stones descend on her own head as often as they reach their goal.

It seems somewhat surprising that the chimpanzees do not make more use of rocks and branches as weapons, since all the mature males we know, and most of the adolescent males, throw things at random to enhance what we call their charging displays. These occur when the chimps become socially excited or frustrated. They rush about wildly, hurling rocks or sticks, dragging branches, slapping the ground or stamping, and leaping into the trees to sway branches violently from side to side.

Faben, during his magnificent displays, often runs upright, holding a stick above his shoulder and then hurling it somewhat as one would a javelin. David Greybeard, whose displays are slow, deliberate, and spectacular, frequently throws large rocks.

Once, when Hugo was in bed with malaria, David arrived behind the tent, stamping and slapping the ground and hooting. In his excitement, he hurled a large stone that by chance went straight toward Hugo, missing his head by a bare two inches. Had it not been for those two inches, Hugo undoubtedly would have had his skull smashed in.

Just as the older apes use rocks, sticks, and other items in displays, so the youngsters use many objects in their games. Besides playing together — wrestling, tickling, or chasing through the trees — young chimps love to play with toys.

Their forest home provides any number of delightful and ingenious playthings which even human children would enjoy. *Strychnos* trees produce round, hard-shelled fruit about the size of tennis balls. The youngsters kick them from foot to hand, or roll them over their bodies.

With the fruit, Figan devised a game of his own: Lying on his back, he spins a *Strychnos* ball round and round, balancing it on his hands and kicking gently with his feet, like a circus bear.

Sometimes the young chimpanzees drag objects along the ground, walking slowly and looking back over their shoulders like children with pull-toys. Fifi once pulled a dead rat by its tail, and Gilka dragged a long stem with a cluster of berries on one end. Fifi found another strange plaything. Once while Hugo was absorbed in taking notes, he heard a

In a "charging display," the excited David Greybeard hurls a rock. Thrown at random, the stone came within inches of Hugo, lying ill with malaria in the tent.

high-pitched noise, glanced casually at Fifi, and returned to his work, thinking she had a whistle.

"Suddenly," he told me afterward, "I realized that Fifi couldn't possibly have a whistle!"

Looking again, he saw that the noise came from a cicada. Fifi held one of its wings in her mouth, and the insect emitted a loud churring sound as it tried to escape.

"Fifi played with it for about half an hour," Hugo told me. "She either held it in her lips, or she put it in the 'groin pocket' between her thigh and abdomen. I could still hear the churring sound in a muffled sort of way. When she apparently had tired of the insect, she looked at it intently, bit off its head, looked at it again, and let it fall to the ground. 'No good any more,' she seemed to say to herself."

Toys like this are not always at hand, but then the youngsters seem just as content to play with stones, leaves, or twigs. They may throw them, rub them over their bodies, pull leaves off stems, break and bend twigs, or poke them into holes in the ground. This form of play may be of tremendous importance in developing dexterity in manipulating objects. As the chimps grow older this skill becomes invaluable not only in routine activities such as nest making and food-gathering, but also in the more specialized field of tool use.

We have never seen an ape under one and a half years of age fish for termites. By the age of three, however, a chimp uses tools as adeptly as adults do. A chimp has the inherent ability to utilize tools because of his hand structure and his well developed brain, but it seems probable that he must learn the tool uses of his community by imitating others.

I remember a day, after Hugo and I returned to the reserve in 1966, when I followed a small chimpanzee group wandering in the forest. During the afternoon the chimps — David Greybeard and Flo, with three of her offspring, Figan, Fifi, and little Flint — headed for the Main Observation Camp.

I trailed after them up the steep track, wondering how I would feel if I were a chimpanzee visiting the camp of the pale-skinned primates for the first time. I would undoubtedly feel apprehensive as I followed David and the others toward the buildings. And I would be terrified at seeing one of the strange upright creatures approaching — covered with some sort of material and with no hair on its arms or legs.

I would recognize the bananas David and the others gathered up with grunts of delight, for a few banana trees grow wild in the reserve. But how could I conceive of fruit growing in concrete boxes on the ground? Definitely, if I were a chimp unfamiliar with the camp, I would remain hidden in the undergrowth, well out of sight. And yet, the fruit would look delicious, and no one would be getting hurt. . . .

The bananas do, in fact, lure the chimpanzees to our feeding area in the Kakombe Stream valley. And the feeding of chimps has, during the past three years, yielded results of scientific significance. In the early years of my study, I learned much of chimpanzee behavior in general, but none of the chimpanzees, in those days, would tolerate my following them. Often I could observe the same individual only once or twice in any one month, and then only when his nomadic travels coincided with my own mountain treks.

TODAY, because of our feeding system, the chimps make a detour and drop in for bananas whenever they wander near our valley. Certain individuals come around almost daily, particularly the older females that do not roam as far as the rest of the chimps. Others call only once a week or once a month. At times nearly all the chimps we know vanish for weeks, going to visit some distant valley, since many of the adults range over the entire reserve and even beyond its boundaries, following no regular circuit. For the most part, however, we can record the behavior of various individuals, the changes in social status, the development of infants.

An ethologist—a scientist who studies animal behavior —finds endless fascination in such details. I must say too that throughout the six-year study of the chimps at the Gombe Stream, I have often felt like an anthropologist taking notes on a tribe of people, for chimpanzees can seem so human.

As I sat that afternoon watching David and the Flo family eating, I thought back over the years that I had known David, and of the major role he had played in the gradual increase of our knowledge. He had been the first of all the chimps to accept me, and his fearless attitude in those early days had done much to influence the behavior of the more timid apes. Later, when Hugo arrived with his cameras and tripods, David's calm acceptance of him again helped the other chimps lose their initial terror.

Incidentally, I owe to David Greybeard my most unforgettable encounter with one of the many other animal inhabitants of the reserve. Late one afternoon, I sat watching him feeding alone in a fig tree. Hearing a slight rustle, I became aware that something fairly large was slowly approaching behind me. I turned, peered into the long grass, and saw a creature with glowing chestnut coat, soft dark eyes, and large inquisitive ears—a female bushbuck.

Timidly she drew nearer, pausing after each step with one foreleg daintily lifted. Poised for flight, her every muscle tensed, she stretched her neck and head toward me. I held my breath as she drew closer and closer until her damp nose actually touched my knee. For me it was a moment of wonder. But the contact terrified her, and she bounded away, her strident alarm bark quickly receding in the distance.

And David not only provided me with my first really significant observation, that wild chimpanzees use and make tools, but back in 1962 he also took the step which led to the establishment of the whole feeding scheme.

It happened this way: One evening, when I was on my own at the reserve, I returned to camp and found Dominic greatly excited. A big male chimpanzee, he said, had come into camp and fed on palm nuts from the tree shading my tent. The next evening Dominic told me the ape had paid another visit.

Hoping he would return, I remained concealed in my tent the next day. Before long David Greybeard stepped into the clearing. With no sign of apprehension he climbed the palm and grunted with pleasure as he poked the red fruits from their horny cups. I could scarcely believe I was actually watching a wild chimpanzee from the veranda of my tent. I wished my mother had been there to share my experience.

David returned every day for about a week while the palm tree continued to yield fruit, and then he stopped coming. But when another of the oil palms fruited, he showed up again. I sometimes waited awhile in camp, hoping to see him before I set off into the mountains. One day, his meal finished, he climbed down, gazed around, and began to walk in his determined manner straight toward me as I sat in the tent veranda. What on earth would he do?

When no more than five feet away, he paused and stared hard at me. I felt uneasy as I watched his hair slowly stand out until he looked twice his true size. This bristling indicates

Staring hard at the author, David snatches a banana from her work table. His daring led Jane to put out fruit to attract other apes to camp.

almost any violent emotion in a chimpanzee — excitement, fear, rage. Suddenly, David rushed forward and grabbed a banana lying on the table!

I asked Dominic to put out the fruit whenever he saw the chimp, and David began dropping by for bananas rather than palm nuts. After some time he actually took a banana from my hand as I held it out to him. He seemed apprehensive, for he stood up and hit the trunk of a tree and rocked from foot to foot, staring at the fruit. But when he took it, there was no snatching. David was amazingly gentle from the first.

A few weeks later, Goliath followed David to camp, and soon he too became a regular visitor. Then William joined the group. William, with his long, scarred upper lip, his timid yet endearing personality, quickly became one of my favorites. It saddened me indeed when two years later he stopped visiting camp. He had suffered for several months from a cough and cold that became steadily worse — chimpanzees appear especially susceptible to respiratory diseases. Although we never found William's body, we are certain that he died, probably of pneumonia.

Soon after William and Goliath first ventured into camp with David, the National Geographic Society sent Hugo to make a photographic record of the chimpanzees' behavior.

Hugo, of Dutch descent, was born in Indonesia, brought up in Australia, England, and the Netherlands, and, like myself, became interested in animals early in life. Once as a boy he made a train journey with two pet foxes that he smuggled aboard in a wicker laundry basket. During the trip the conductor opened the carriage door.

"What on earth is that terrible smell?" he asked, taking Hugo's ticket. His gaze came to rest suspiciously on the basket.

"Oh, that's just dirty washing," replied Hugo innocently, pushing the contraband farther under the seat. The conductor gave him a long, hard look as he left, closing the door firmly behind him.

Hugo's first filming experience, at the age of 14, perhaps influenced his decision to make animal photography a career. He and some friends decided to photograph wild sheep in Holland. In those days Hugo was ignorant of the mysteries of the camera. Terms like shutter speed, depth of field, and diaphragm meant nothing to him. Nevertheless, his friends considered him the most likely to succeed in getting close enough to the wary sheep to film them with a short lens, the only one they possessed. So with the camera pre-set for him by his companions, Hugo crept toward the sheep and pressed the button. The results were all that could be desired.

In 1959 Hugo's interest in animals led him, as mine had led me, to Africa. He had been working for a motion-picture firm in Holland. In Africa he joined a television company, filming animals for two years, then began work as a freelance photographer. At that point Dr. Leakey influenced Hugo's life—just as he had influenced mine a couple of years earlier. The National Geographic Society wanted a motion-picture record of Dr. Leakey's work at Olduvai Gorge, and Hugo made the film. Dr. Leakey then suggested that Hugo be given the chance to photograph the chimpanzees at the Gombe Stream Game Reserve.

We had been expecting Hugo's arrival for some days when, one August evening in 1962, I returned to camp and found him surrounded by piles of equipment.

"I didn't like to put up my tent," he said, after we had greeted each other. "For I got your note saying that chimps were coming to camp, and I wasn't sure whether they'd be scared of a new one."

I wasn't sure either, but after discussing the problem we selected a spot where we thought the chimpanzees would least notice another tent. David Greybeard arrived early the next morning and Hugo remained hidden inside. David fed

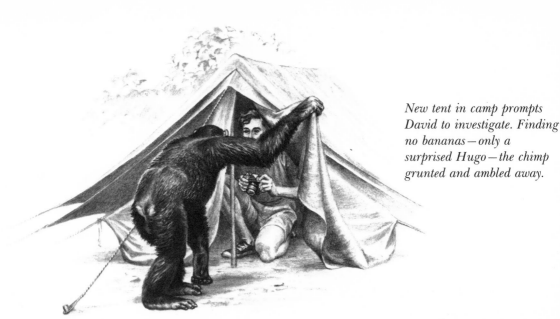

New tent in camp prompts David to investigate. Finding no bananas—only a surprised Hugo—the chimp grunted and ambled away.

on bananas with scarcely a glance in the direction of the new tent. His meal finished, he decided to investigate.

"I was looking through the flap," Hugo said afterward, "and I held my breath as I saw him coming straight toward me. I thought he'd get a frightful shock if he saw me inside."

But David, after lifting the canvas and peering into the tent, merely grunted—no bananas there—and wandered away. Hugo, however, had his camera ready and was able to photograph a chimpanzee on his first morning at the camp!

When William and Goliath became accustomed to Hugo and his equipment, he filmed sequences of the interactions among the three chimps. But he had to get shots of the other apes as well, and this proved much more difficult, for they feared the stranger as much as they had once feared me.

Near fruit trees where I hoped the chimps would go to feed, we built small blinds—simple tangles of palm fronds and other vegetation. In these Hugo would wait, hour after hour, perched on uncomfortably steep slopes, pestered by ants, hoping chimpanzees would come. When they did approach they invariably spotted his camera lens peeping from the blind, stared in terror, then fled silently into the forest. Gradually, however, the apes lost their fear. David Greybeard hastened the process, for sometimes when he spied Hugo and me in the mountains he would leave his group and wander over to see if we had a banana for him. Or, failing that, he would attempt to steal a piece of clothing—for all the chimpanzees love to suck and chew on things and are especially fond of cloth or cardboard.

Once, in full view of his fellow apes, David tried to

take a sweater that was a favorite of Hugo's. To save it I gave David a worn one of mine. He carried the trophy back to his wide-eyed companions, and they immediately gathered round to beg for scraps of wool.

Not long after that incident, a large group of chimps climbed into a fig tree, stared hard at Hugo's camera lens, relaxed, and started to feed. Hugo thought his luck had changed. Yet that night he returned to camp gloomy and depressed, cold and soaked to the skin.

"It all seemed perfect," he told my mother, who had returned to the reserve for another few months. "The lighting couldn't have been better. I was frantically filming when, after about five minutes, a black cloud covered the sun. Rain began to pour, and I could scarcely see the chimps, let alone film them. They fed there for two hours while I sat shivering, with a polyethylene bag over my camera, praying for sun."

To make it even worse, he had waited at that tree for five days before the chimps appeared — and during that time not even the smallest cloud floated over. The same thing happened again and again: While he waited, the sun shone; when chimps arrived, the rain began.

It seemed, indeed, as though photography at the Gombe Stream was destined to be spoiled by rain. Previously, at the end of 1961, my sister Judy had joined me to try to get pictures of the chimps. Day after day she crouched in pouring rain under a sheet of polyethylene. Nonetheless, she was well rewarded for all her discomfort: She got the first pictures of chimps fishing for termites.

Despite the downpours, Hugo had secured so much excellent film material by the end of the year that the National Geographic Society thought it worthwhile to send him back in 1963 for nine months of additional filming.

That same year David Greybeard arrived in camp with the old female Flo and her family — Fifi, a three-year-old, Figan, a juvenile, and Faben, an adolescent. This event turned out to be the second major step in the development of the chimpanzee feeding scheme. Flo became a frequent visitor, and we grew to love her wonderfully ugly features — the bulbous, deformed nose, the drooping lower lip.

In July, after three years of maternal preoccupation with Fifi, Flo again became attractive to the males. A whole retinue of suitors followed her to camp one day, with several

Nesting at midday 30 feet above ground
two apes escape the damp forest floor during the rain
season. Jane watches from waist-high grass

youngsters and females tagging along. After these newcomers
found courage to leave the undergrowth for a banana, they
soon learned to return for more.

At that point, with 20 chimpanzees of both sexes and
various ages visiting camp, it became worthwhile to organize
the feeding scheme on a permanent basis. But what a struggle
we had in setting it up! For one thing, David quickly discovered
our main banana supply down on the beach near Dominic's
and Hassan's quarters.

Hassan had built a structure of strong wooden bars
thickly covered with grass, and he assured us proudly that no
chimpanzee could steal from *that* store. But David made a hole
in the roof in a matter of minutes, and while we looked on
helplessly he remained inside, gorging himself. Even though
he had to enlarge the hole to get out, he nevertheless dragged
a large bunch after him when he staggered into the undergrowth. After that we erected an aluminum building to protect the bananas.

A T THE FEEDING AREA ITSELF, our idea was to give each
chimpanzee a ration of ten to fifteen bananas. But how
could we fix boxes in which to safeguard these shares? Every
type we tried the chimpanzees opened either by brute strength
or manipulative cunning. They pulled pegs, opened catches,
yanked cords. The adult males wanted everybody else's share
for themselves—and David had shown us that each one could
eat as many as 60 bananas at one sitting.

We finally devised concrete boxes with steel lids held
shut by wires threaded through underground pipes and
attached to levers some distance away. When a lever is released, the wire becomes slack and the lid falls open. But even
the concrete boxes were by no means the ultimate solution.
Some of the youngsters learned to pull out the pins that lock
the levers, and when we substituted tight nuts and bolts for
the simple pins, they learned to unscrew those. Now we plan
to install electrically operated boxes, the lid of each to fall
open when we press a button inside the building. Still, we
sometimes wonder if our own ingenuity will ever surpass that
of these clever chimpanzees.

However, it is their ability to reason, their skill in manip-
ulation, and their sophisticated use of natural objects that
make them such fascinating subjects for study.

6

5

4

KASEKERA

THE PEAK

1

2

TRAIL

3

KAKOMBE STREAM

Growing research community in the Kakombe Stream valley reflects a courageous young scientist's progress in her continuing study of apes in the wild. Since 1960, when the author began her work near the tiny lakeshore settlement of Kasekera, she has twice moved and enlarged her camp. From the Peak she first observed chimpanzees at close range. Now, by supplying bananas, she attracts her subjects to the Main Observation Camp.

KEY TO ILLUSTRATION:
1. MAIN OBSERVATION CAMP   4. LAKE CAMP
2. BANANA STOREROOM   5. STAFF QUARTERS
3. RIDGE CAMP   6. BOATHOUSE

Fishing for termites, Gombe Stream chimps demonstrate the ability to fashion and use crude tools—a skill long believed to set man apart from all other animals. The apes, by stripping leaves from twigs and trimming the edges from blades of grass, make fishing rods for probing the mounds. When the insects bite, the anglers carefully withdraw the stems and pick off the food with their lips. Too young to fish, Flint clings to mother Flo as sister Fifi concentrates

on her work. Shy Marina (upper right) usually dines alone. Flint watches closely (right) as Flo explores an opening she made by scratching away the thin layer of soil termites use to seal their burrows. By the age of three, youngsters can use such tools as expertly as their elders.

Ardent angler, Fifi seeks an opening in a termite mound by bending low for a close look and a quick sniff. After breaking into a narrow tunnel sealed by clay, she inserts a blade of grass. Her average catch: half a dozen of the forest delicacies. Patient chimpanzees capture scores of insects at a single sitting.

Termites spice the menu, but virtually all the chimpanzees' food grows on trees. Among the branches, apes dine on fruit, leaves, seeds, bark, and resin.

Ingenuity provides a drink for a thirsty ape. Finding rainwater cupped in a fallen tree, but out of reach of his lips, Figan manufactures a "sponge." First he briefly chews a few leaves to increase their absorbency, then dips the crumpled greenery into the natural bowl and sucks out the liquid. By fashioning a simple tool he saves himself the bother of walking to a stream for a drink.

African boys shyly greet the author at her lakeshore camp. Here in
1962 the young scientist made her first close acquaintance
with a wild chimpanzee. Attracted by fruiting oil palms, David Greybeard
calmly entered the camp, climbed a tree, and began feeding. Jane
proffered bananas, and eventually the ape accepted one from her hand.

Crusty J. B. thrusts out his jaw.

Mr. McGregor, "old man of the forest."

Timid Olly avoids companions.

Spiteful Melissa harbors grudges.

Leakey, rugged but gentle (opposite, lower left);
white chin distinguishes David Greybeard.

Family portrait: Flo relaxes with baby Flint, young Fifi, and adolescent Figan.

Camera captivates Fifi, who spoils Baron van Lawick's plans for a close-up when she sees her image in the lens and cranes her neck for a better view. With the camera on the ground, she crouches for a close-up of her own.

Filming in the rain, Hugo shields his movie equipment with an umbrella. The photographer began recording chimpanzee behavior at the Gombe Stream Reserve in 1962. In the wet season, he wages a constant battle to keep moisture from ruining film and cameras.

Banana Club, begun casually by the author, meets every day around concrete containers filled with these chimps' favorite fruit. David Greybeard's early visits with Jane gave her the idea of using bananas to attract the chimps. Now a permanent feeding system keeps them coming to camp, allowing the young scientist to make daily observations of chimpanzee behavior and record baby Flint's development. Three months old and not yet on solid food, the infant sits in Flo's lap and nibbles a finger. Above, Flint lolls on his mother's back as she gazes longingly at the food in Mike's mouth.

MANTIS (POLYSPILOTA AERUGINOSA), 1 1/2 TIMES LIFE-SIZE

FIRE BALL LILY (HAEMANTHUS MULTIFLORUS), 1/2 LIFE-SIZE

MILK PODS (DIPLORHYNCHUS CONDYLOCARPON)

GEOMETER MOTH (PROBLEPSIS SP.), TWICE LIFE-SIZE

MALLOW (HIBISCUS SP.), 1 1/2 TIMES LIFE-SIZE

BRACONID WASP LARVAE (APANTELES SP.) CONSUME A CATERPILLAR. TWICE LIFE-SIZE

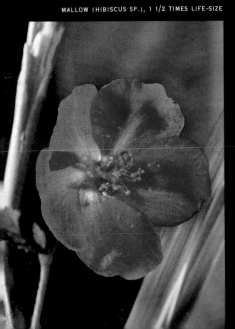

ID BUG NYMPH (FAMILY FLATIDAE), 4 TIMES LIFE-SIZE

LARVA OF A NOCTUID MOTH (RHANIDOPHORA SP.), 2 1/2 TIMES LIFE-SIZE

BIDENS STEPPIA, SLIGHTLY SMALLER THAN LIFE-SIZE

Hidden world of the Gombe Stream: Lethe wasp moth emerges from its cocoon, and a tiny flatid bug nymph perches on a stem. Filaments churning, a caterpillar hunches along a twig. A mantis cleans its leg, and a geometer moth silvers a leaf. On slopes and valleys bloom yellow-petaled *Bidens steppia*, purple-tinged *Asystasia*, the fire ball lily, and the radiant hibiscus. Chimpanzees savor the brown milk pods.

TASIA GANGETICA, 1 1/3 TIMES LIFE-SIZE

LETHE WASP MOTH (EUCHROMIA LETHE), TWICE LIFE-SIZE

*Tight-lipped with
ferocity, Rodolf kills
a baboon for
food by smashing
it against the ground
while his companions scream
in a frenzy of excitement.*

3

Days for Hunting, Days for Rain

"HUGO! THEY'VE GOT ONE!" I called, shouting above the bedlam of chimpanzee screams and the barking and screeching of a troop of baboons. At 8:40 in the morning, on hearing a sudden commotion just down the slope from the camp, I had rushed out in time to see Rodolf, our largest male chimpanzee, in the act of killing a young baboon—holding it by one leg and bashing its head against the ground.

Grabbing a camera, Hugo joined me as the ape, his hair on end, flung the body in front of him, his face awful in its ferocity. Three other chimpanzees with him screamed loudly and threw their arms around one another, so intensely agitated that they seemed no more than a black, hairy tangle of bodies, arms, and legs.

Rodolf seized his prey in one hand and set off up the mountainside, with the other chimpanzees trailing him closely as he pushed his way through the tall grass. Most of the baboons had already disappeared from the scene of slaughter, but a few of the big males had remained. Enraged, they slapped the ground with their hands and lunged forward with threatening barks as Rodolf passed with the limp body of their troop member. But none attacked him.

I had first seen a chimpanzee eating meat—a young bushpig—in 1960. Until then many people believed wild chimps were almost exclusively vegetarian, perhaps occasionally supplementing their diet with insects or a fledgling bird or small rodent. The fact that they do, in some areas anyway, prey on larger animals—such as young bushbuck and bushpig, and various types of monkey—came to light, so far as I can determine, during my research.

Now Hugo and I struggled up the steep slope, following the path taken by Rodolf and the others. Suddenly Hugo pointed. "There they are!" he said, indicating a tall *miombo* tree. Among the topmost branches sat Rodolf with his kill. As we sought a place for Hugo to set up his camera, we heard the calls of several chimpanzee groups, drawing closer as they hurried toward the tree, hoping to share in the feast. By the time we found a good vantage point, ten more chimpanzees had arrived, including the top-ranking Mike, his powerful friend J. B., and the once-supreme Goliath.

NOTHING COULD DEMONSTRATE more clearly a human-like acknowledgement of the rights of ownership than their behavior that day. Mike, J. B., and Goliath all held a higher social rank than Rodolf; yet as they gathered around the hunter they simply gazed longingly at the red meat, making no attempt to wrest it away.

Tentatively, Mike reached toward the kill. Rodolf, who normally goes into a frenzy of submission if Mike merely approaches, pulled the prize away. Goliath held his hand to Rodolf's mouth, begging for the flesh he was chewing. Rodolf pushed his hand away roughly.

Later in the morning, more chimps arrived, some going close to beg and some watching from afar, each according to status. High and low alike watched hungrily as Rodolf, his prey held firmly between thigh and belly, pulled off bits of flesh. He followed each bite of meat with a mouthful of leaves, chewing them together.

Rodolf selfishly guarded his feast. True, he allowed Mike and J. B., Goliath and Huxley, to take small pieces from time to time, but we never saw him place bits of meat in their outstretched hands, as I once had seen Huxley do. And when Mr. McGregor reached up and took hold of a piece of the dangling viscera, it was only by luck that it tumbled into his eager hands.

If other chimpanzees dared approach, Mike, Goliath, or J. B. chased them away. These three males, held back from taking the baboon from one normally their inferior, vented their frustrations on others of lower rank.

By noon, Rodolf looked comfortably full. His paunch,

large enough at the best of times, bulged even more as he climbed down the tree and walked a short distance with the kill slung over his shoulder, looking like some hairy prehistoric man after a successful hunt. The others followed and gathered around him as he reclined in the shade.

For a while all was peaceful. Rodolf lay replete, while Mike tore contentedly at the liver he had managed somehow to get all to himself, and Goliath chewed a piece of flesh. J. B. had left the group temporarily, slipping down to camp for a quick snack of bananas.

Fifi and her infant brother Flint played in the vines overhead, and old Flo lay stretched out on the ground, her nose almost touching the carcass. Although Rodolf had made the kill four hours before, much of the meat remained. The softer abdomen, one leg, and part of a shoulder were gone. The rest had scarcely been touched—partly because chimpanzees always eat meat very slowly, partly because Rodolf had shared so little of his feast.

The afternoon wore on. Rodolf, like a child stuffed with candy but unable to resist one more piece, sat up and again picked at the kill. The others promptly gathered around to resume begging. Now and then the undergrowth exploded with black hurtling bodies, and piercing screams broke the peace as Mike or Goliath charged at some subordinate who approached too closely.

J. B. gave me one nasty moment. He bustled up the track from camp, hurried toward Rodolf, then suddenly saw me crouching in the undergrowth. He stood quite still, staring, and his hair rose. For a moment he swooshed a branch violently from side to side, then with a terrifying yell and a fierce gleam in his eyes charged toward me. The thick undergrowth prevented my escape and I stayed completely still, my heart beating uncomfortably fast and my thoughts frozen.

J. B. gave my leg a terrific wham, stopped in front of me, and with frenzied hands grabbed at the dark sweater on the ground beside me. Feverishly he sniffed it and touched it with his lips and tongue, only to discard it and subject my notebook and then my camera to the same treatment. After that he turned his back and hurried away to beg from Rodolf. I can only suppose that, in the dim light, he thought I had managed to get a share of the meat—and that, of course, he could not have tolerated!

At 3:30 in the afternoon, Rodolf put the kill over his shoulder and set off down the slope, followed by a few of the most persistent beggars—Mike and J. B., Goliath and Huxley, and David, a later arrival. Rodolf walked to the stream and, holding the carcass tightly in his groin, bent down and sucked up his fill of the cool, clear water. Then, still keeping a firm hold on his prey, he stretched out on the ground while the other chimps sat around grooming one another.

Fifteen minutes later Rodolf sat up. He looked at the remains of the baboon, raised it to his mouth, and pulled off a tiny scrap of flesh. Suddenly he abandoned the carcass, moved about ten feet away, and sat down. Never will Hugo and I forget the scene that followed. For a few moments the other chimps stared without moving, as though unable to believe the long wait had ended. Then all together they converged on the meat, grabbing and pulling and screaming.

Mike, presumably because he could not seize the entire prize, leaped onto the backs of the scrabbling mob and attacked one and all alike, stamping on them and pulling their hair. His ferocious assault won him what remained, and he charged away, flailing the meat up and down as he ran. The others, however, were not to be thwarted—not even by Mike. Like hounds after a fox they pursued him, and when they caught up they grabbed at the carcass.

They pulled and tore and screamed until after a few minutes each emerged from the fray with a share. Not very equal shares though—Mike had the head and shoulders, David the tender rump, and the other three got only small pieces. Rodolf, after quietly watching the performance, ambled away to sleep off his feast.

HUXLEY, GOLIATH, AND J. B. soon finished their bits of meat, scraping the last vestige of tendon from the bone and biting open the ends to get at the marrow. Then Mike, with the beneficence of a generous sovereign, allowed the three to take some of his portion. David greedily turned his back on all beggars until, much later, he allowed Goliath a share, tearing off a tender red morsel to place in the outstretched hand of his friend.

In the coolness of evening we saw perhaps the most gruesome sight of the day. Mike stopped feeding for a few moments, lay on his back in the last of the sunlight and,

holding the baboon head above him with one foot, groomed the fur of his trophy—not once but time and time again.

But, almost as though to make up for this horrific incident, the day ended with pure slapstick comedy. While Mike sat relaxed, idly picking at the remains of the head, J. B. lay stretched out nearby, looking fat and full. Suddenly, he seemed to explode—one moment he was there, the next he had streaked past Mike and disappeared in the long grass. Mike stared after him, a surprised look on his face. Hugo and I, startled for a moment, burst out laughing when we realized that J. B. had accomplished the neatest thievery of all—the head of the baboon had vanished from Mike's hands!

When the other chimps wandered away we again caught sight of J. B. In a nest high in a nearby tree, he was dining on stolen baboon.

After returning to camp, Hugo and I told the others about the day's events.

"How often do these chimps eat meat?" Michael asked.

"Much more often than I used to think," I replied. "I've seen them eating it 18 times altogether and we've also learned, by examining dung samples every day, that in one year no less than 23 animals were eaten—and there must have been many more that we never knew about."

"Most of their prey seems to be red colobus monkey,

Powerful arm upraised, J. B. charges the author. Striking her savagely on the leg, he grabbed her belongings and sniffed them, apparently believing them part of the baboon killed earlier by Rodolf.

Banded mongooses scratch among dead leaves and rotting wood for snails, mice, insects, and snakes. Roaming the reserve in packs, the small, keen-sighted mammals twitter when pleased, bark when alarmed.

young bushbuck, and young bushpig," Hugo added. "And it seems that the chimps eat only animals they kill themselves. Once we offered them a freshly killed bushpig but none of them, except one small infant, so much as licked at it. They just stared at the carcass and seemed rather frightened."

Prior to Rodolf's kill we had seen chimpanzees eating baboon only twice, but several times we had seen them hunting young baboons. On one such occasion, Hugo and I sat watching a group of chimps resting in the shade of a tall fig tree. In its branches, a juvenile baboon fed alone, separated by some 200 yards from the rest of his troop. Presently Huxley plodded up from the stream toward the peaceful chimpanzee group. About ten feet from the fig tree he stopped, facing its trunk. To us he seemed unaware even of the existence of the small baboon above. Nonetheless, as though he had in fact given a signal, the other chimps stood up. Two of the males moved to the base of the fig tree; three others stationed themselves under two nearby trees, the branches of which formed an escape route for the baboon. And then, very slowly and with infinite caution, Figan, the youngest of the males present (he was about eight at the time), began to creep toward his quarry.

But the baboon spotted Figan when he had approached to within 15 feet. With a shrill bark, it sped away through the branches. Figan followed, but the cry had alerted the other baboons in the troop and they hurried to the scene. A noisy and dramatic encounter followed: Baboons and chimps screamed and barked and leaped at one another. But the battle consisted of threat and bluff. So far as we could tell, neither side inflicted wounds on the other. During the uproar, however, the chimps' quarry escaped.

Ten minutes later the baboons moved away, and the chimpanzees returned to the shade of the fig tree. To this day we do not understand how Huxley so effectively conveyed to the other chimpanzees his desire to hunt. In general, such hunts seemed more a matter of opportunity than of habit, as I reported in 1964 to the National Geographic Society's Committee for Research and Exploration, in Washington, D.C.

A FTER MY VISIT to the United States that year, I went to London, where Hugo and I were married the day before Easter. The church blossomed with yellow daffodils and white arum lilies. Our bridesmaids were eight-year-old Alison Davis, granddaughter of Dr. Leakey, and Virginia Coryndon, nine, granddaughter of Sir Robert Coryndon, who founded the museum in Nairobi where I first met Dr. Leakey. Unfortunately, Dr. Leakey could not attend, but he sent a wedding speech on tape from America.

Hugo and I limited our honeymoon to three days because we had received letters from Dominic and from the young Polish-born mycologist Kristopher Pirozynski, who was looking after the camp in our absence, telling us that Flo had given birth. We hurried back to Africa, for little Flint, as we later named Flo's offspring, offered us our first opportunity to record the development of a wild chimpanzee infant.

We arrived in Nairobi, alas, during the heavy rains, when many East African roads are impassable. Our route to Kigoma, we had been assured, would be all right so long as we journeyed by Land-Rover with its four-wheel drive. But with three-quarters of the trip from Nairobi and two flooded rivers behind us, we found the road hopelessly blocked by deep water. We had no choice but to turn back.

Wearily Hugo wheeled the Land-Rover about, and at once we saw a new danger. Not far away, rain fell in torrents from jet-black clouds. Fifteen miles of treacherous road lay between us and the first of the rivers we must recross.

"If either of the other rivers rises much, we shall really be stuck," Hugo warned, pressing his foot down urgently on the accelerator. "We may not be able to cross for days, or even weeks—perhaps not until the end of the rainy season."

Hugo drove as fast as possible through the dreary, tsetse-fly-infested forest as the rain pelted down. Finally we reached the first river and found to our relief that the water had risen only a couple of inches. But a tricky crossing confronted us, for the road, which lay hidden by the floodwaters, curved sharply where it joined the bridge. As on our earlier crossing, I stood knee-deep in water, marking the bend for Hugo, and then at the last moment splashed ahead of the car as fast as I could.

Three miles farther on we reached the second river, now dangerously high. Hugo looked at me questioningly: "Shall we risk it?" I nodded, for the thought of being stranded in that gloomy, deserted country appalled me. Hugo drove full speed into the water. About halfway across, the engine faltered and the wheels slipped sideways on the hidden bridge. Panic gripped us as we felt the raging current push against the Land-Rover. Then mercifully the engine picked up and we reached the opposite bank. Hugo and I felt vastly relieved that no more flooded rivers lay ahead!

We drove the Land-Rover another 100 miles back the way we had come, then put our equipment on a train bound for Kigoma and got aboard. Before finally reaching the little port town, we spent a long night swaying about among all our gear inside the Land-Rover on a railway flatcar.

AFTER OUR ARRIVAL only one more train got through to Kigoma in the next three months, for heavy rains blocked road and rail traffic that year. The level of Lake Tanganyika rose, and the water flooded the harbor facilities. The stores ran out of one thing after another: tea and sugar, coffee and milk, kerosene and potatoes. By the time a train chugged through water as much as three feet deep to reach Kigoma, we were on meager rations.

In this part of the world, the rainy season begins in October or November and continues until April or May. Week after week the skies remain gray and thick, with misty clouds swirling over the mountain peaks or hanging motionless above the forested slopes. Downpours may come at any moment, and the streams become torrents as soil-reddened water hurtles down the valleys with frightening force, rolling huge boulders as it goes.

When the sun does appear, it draws moisture from the rain-soaked forests and the mountains seem rather like an overheated tropical greenhouse. On most days, however, at least one heavy rainstorm occurs, and sometimes water pours from a leaden sky for as long as 12 hours without letup.

The beat of rain on a canvas tent—when one lies cozily in bed—makes a most delightful sound, but the enjoyment passes quickly when one arises in the morning to find the ditches around the tent overflowing and the floor inches deep in water. Even our new buildings have flooded in particularly heavy rainstorms.

During the rains, we constantly battle to keep the water from ruining our equipment. Moisture condenses in binoculars, clothing stays damp, ball-point pens refuse to mark the soggy pages of our notebooks, and typewriter keys stick.

Everywhere hangs the faint, musty odor of mildew. Hugo must wipe camera lenses daily to keep them free of a fungus that etches and clouds glass. The damp causes film to catch in his movie cameras, tripod legs become almost too stiff to move, and moisture endangers precious exposed film.

On the whole, though, I love the reserve in the rainy season, particularly the forest. The wet undergrowth and rotting wood and leaves give off a pungent smell, the vegetation gleams, and all around I hear the sound of rain. Then I can move soundlessly, with no rustling or crackling to betray me to the shy forest creatures.

Many times I have crept close to a hunting party of 15 or more banded mongooses poking and prying into every nook

Devilish chimp gnaws on a manuscript, and wins himself a name—Satan. In a futile effort to distract him, Hugo offers his socks and the shirt off his back.

and cranny, chattering continuously as they passed me in a long, straggling line. And I have watched the long-nosed elephant shrew, with its fawn-and-black striped body, catching insects in the wet leaves. These small, agile animals hunt by smacking their slender tails against the ground and then snapping up the insects that scuttle from their hiding places.

ONCE, WHILE PUSHING THROUGH the dripping forest during my first rainy season at the reserve, I became aware of a black form, a chimpanzee, hunched on a low branch. I stopped quickly, sat on the sodden ground, and pretended to busy myself with my own concerns—for the chimps do not like for us to stare at them. Then I heard a slight sound behind me and, looking around, saw two eyes glaring through the undergrowth from beneath heavy brows.

Next, a rustle caused me to look to my right where I saw a black hand, its huge fingers curled around a vine. I was surrounded. All sound ceased except for the dripping of the rain. Suddenly the hand moved, shaking the vine with jerky, threatening motions. Then stillness again. A movement above made me glance up, and there I saw another male almost directly overhead. As I looked, he too shook a branch.

Then came a low-pitched, worried "hoo," repeated again and again—now behind me, now to the right, now above —the sounds of uneasy chimpanzees. Silence again. It was uncanny and nerve-racking, and had I been engaged on any other mission than that of studying these creatures, I would undoubtedly have hurried away. Instead, I sat and waited.

With startling violence the apes began to threaten in earnest. Everywhere, branches shook, and around me rose the aggressive "wraaa" call—a drawn-out, high-pitched cry that I consider one of the most savage sounds of the African forests. Above my head the big male rocked a sapling until a branch actually bumped my head.

All at once, as though at a signal, quiet returned. I heard no slightest movement. Only when I looked around did I discover that the glaring eyes, the huge hand, and the black shape above had vanished. I was alone. I must confess that when I stood up, my knees felt weak beneath me!

To all outward appearances the chimpanzees dislike the rain. At the beginning of a heavy storm they often seek shelter beneath a thick tangle of vegetation or a leaning tree trunk. But once the water drips through their "roof," they usually move into the open and sit looking cold and miserable, with heads bowed, chins tucked in, and knees drawn up to their chests. When they move from place to place, they often walk upright, arms held close to their bodies, one hand clasping the wrist of the other, as though they cannot bear to place their hands on the wet ground.

We always feel particularly sorry for them when it rains hard at night, while we lie snug beneath a sheltering roof. If they sleep near camp, we hear a chorus of melancholy hoots when the rain begins, and we picture the poor chimps hunched in their nests, cold and shivering. Even after the rain stops, they have only a sodden platform of leaves to lie on for the rest of the night.

Until they are about a year old, infants probably fare the best in a deluge, for their mothers protect them with body, arms, and legs. While Flint was small, we often noticed that even after the longest storm he emerged virtually dry when Flo stretched out her cramped limbs.

The older offspring frequently keep warm by frenzied activity, chasing one another through the trees or playing alone. Fifi in particular often rushes about by herself during heavy rain, leaping from branch to branch, hanging, twirling, and twisting from one hand, waving her arms around while dangling by her feet, or swinging round a tree, brandishing a branch in her hand. Once we watched Figan in his younger days turn somersault after somersault, until we felt quite dizzy. At the end of this bloodwarming exercise he sat on the wet ground in the pouring rain, his hair ruffled and covered with mud, looking a trifle dizzy himself!

Nor do the adult male chimpanzees always sit huddled and passive in the rain. Sometimes when the first drops hit them they begin a display, wildly and rhythmically swaying from foot to foot, rocking saplings to and fro, stamping the ground. This spectacular performance we call a "rain dance."

Chimpanzees may also respond in the same way to high wind and to a particularly stimulating social situation, but it is typically their reaction to a sudden downpour. On two occasions I saw group performances of these rain dances. The first will always haunt my memory.

The spectacle began as I sat watching a number of chimps feeding and playing in a tree on the opposite slope of

Hungry horde of apes pursues Hugo as he races toward a new feeding area half a mile from the old. As bait he carries a single banana—and an empty box.

a narrow ravine. Rain had threatened all morning, and finally it came down. The chimps climbed from the tree and moved up the grassy slope. Seemingly by chance, they divided into two groups, with four adult males in one and three in the other.

As they neared the ridge, one of the males turned suddenly and charged diagonally downward, slapping the ground and barking loudly. At once a male from the other group turned and began to charge too. Standing upright, he tore a low branch from a tree, waved it above his head for a moment, then dragged it behind him as he rushed down the slope.

Meanwhile, near the skyline, the females and youngsters had climbed trees where they sat and watched the wild display. At the top of the slope another male stood upright, his arms swinging slightly, his hair on end. Then he too plunged down the hill, breaking off a great bough on his way. Two more set off, hooting wildly.

One after the other the males sprang into a tree and, without a pause, hurled themselves to the ground, tearing off branches as they fell and dragging them as they charged. At the bottom some of the apes grabbed tree trunks to break their headlong rush. Others swung into the branches and sat for a moment, silent and still, before climbing down to plod back to the top, where they turned to charge again.

All the time the rain pelted down as lightning streaked the dark sky. The crash of thunder all but drowned out the wild calls of the apes. Against the green grass, they looked black and very large, like primitive men displaying their strength and defying the elements. While I watched I found it hard to remember that as a scientist I should interpret this strange behavior in scientific terms.

After half an hour the amazing display ended. The actors trudged up to the ridge, the spectators climbed from their trees, and one by one the chimpanzees disappeared over the top, leaving the hillside empty and deserted in the rain. Only the torn branches and the fresh white scars on the tree trunks remained to show that the wild performance had not been some figment of my imagination.

S OON after Hugo and I returned to the reserve in 1964, Edna Koning joined us as our first assistant. A Dutch girl, she had been living with her parents in Peru. The year before, with an ever-increasing number of chimpanzees visiting the feeding area, I had been hard pressed to cope with the work—the observation, recording, and typing. Often I worked late into the night to keep up to date with the events of the crowded days. Edna took over the typing and helped in many other ways as well. I was even able to complete some analyses of data for a section of my thesis.

Near the end of 1964, when the number of chimps visiting camp had reached 45, we employed another assistant, Sonia Ivey, who had worked as a secretary in England. She arrived in November, and my mother, at the reserve on her third visit, went to Kigoma to meet her.

When they returned, there were no fewer than 30 chimpanzees in the camp. The apes were still shy of strangers, so we quickly concealed Sonia inside a tent. She looked completely bewildered.

"But you don't mean to say you can recognize all of them?" she said. "They look exactly alike to me."

A month later Sonia wondered how she could have been so imperceptive. How could *anyone* confuse Mike with J. B., or David with Goliath! Yet most of our visitors to the reserve react the same way when they first see the chimps.

In May, 1964, we decided to move the feeding area. I felt sad in a way to leave the Lake Camp, the place where four years earlier my mother and I had first pitched our tent. We thought, however, that the more timid chimps would feel bolder if we placed the camp farther up the valley and away from the bustle of the fishermen on the beach. We set up the new Ridge Camp at night to avoid disturbing the chimpanzees with the comings and goings of the Africans we hired to carry our belongings.

Everything was ready at last, and on one memorable day Hugo led 15 chimpanzees from the old camp to the new — a distance of more than half a mile. He achieved this by showing David Greybeard a banana and a box in which we often kept the fruit. Then Hugo set off at a run up the steep slope, over a ridge, and down the track to the new site. Although Hugo had not been very hopeful of success, David followed at once, screaming in delighted anticipation. The other chimps rushed along behind. In the new camp, I heard the bedlam of calls and hastily flung out bananas to the excited horde.

"My one horror," Hugo confessed as he lay sprawled exhausted on the ground, "was that the chimps would catch up and find out that I was cheating. That box was empty!"

The other chimpanzees quickly discovered the new feeding place and, as we had predicted, even the timid ones became more relaxed and confident. At the old camp it was they who had ventured into our territory; now it was we who invaded theirs. Observation became increasingly easy, for we could move around freely without upsetting our subjects.

N OTHER WAYS, though, life became increasingly difficult. For even the shyest of the chimps, as they lost their fear of humans, plucked up courage to enter our tents—and each was a prospective thief. Every morning we bundled all our clothes and bedding into large wooden crates. Woe betide any of us careless enough to leave a garment lying around.

Nor had the chimps lost their passion for chewing cardboard and cloth. J. B. once made off with a box full of groceries. We followed a trail of jars and tins until finally we came to the tree where the thief sat peacefully chewing the cardboard. Six other chimps from time to time held their hands to his mouth in the hope that he would allow them to

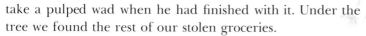

*Tug-of-war between Hugo and David
ends in a tie — almost. The photographer
saved his camera, but the chimp got
part of the shirt used to camouflage the lens.*

take a pulped wad when he had finished with it. Under the tree we found the rest of our stolen groceries.

One day, a young chimp we had never seen before got hold of a chapter of a novel my mother was writing. We had hidden inside a tent (the ritual when new chimps appear) and we found ourselves at a loss as to how to retrieve it. The youngster — named Satan then and there — scampered away with the sheaf of papers and began chewing on one corner.

Valiantly Hugo flung out his sweater, even his shirt and socks, in the hope that one of the other chimps might take a garment and distract Satan's attention from his prize. But the stratagem failed. Fortunately the chapter proved rather tasteless to young Satan and after some tense moments he bounded away, leaving the papers almost intact.

Hugo has lost more than one shirt to the chimps. One morning, while he was concealed in a camera blind, David Greybeard ambled up and stopped just in front of him.

"I wondered what on earth he was doing," Hugo said afterward. "Suddenly to my horror I saw my camera disappearing through the hole in the blind! I grabbed it and then realized that David was pulling on the shirt that I'd draped over the lens to try to camouflage it." So Hugo and David had a tug-of-war that ended with the shirt tearing and David plodding off triumphantly with his half.

I think Kristopher Pirozynski, during the four months he looked after the camp for us, suffered most from this strange craving of the chimps to chew on our belongings. His work of collecting the micro-fungi which grow on plants took him out on daily trips into the reserve, and the African staff worked too far from his tent to notice every time the chimps came around. By the time Hugo and I reached the reserve,

Baby Flint emerges virtually dry from
his mother's arms after a cloudburst. Chimps
dislike the rain, yet never make shelters

Kris's belongings were sadly depleted, and indeed we had
only to look around the camp to see evidence of the chimps'
destructive habits.

"One of their oddest crazes was for objects made of
wood," Kris told us. "For a couple of weeks they all sat round
chewing it." He pointed to the row of backless, nibbled shelves
standing on the veranda.

N EXT CAME a passion for canvas. The hairy vandals tore
strips from tent flaps, removed and chewed the canvas
from Kris's chair, and made off with two pairs of gym shoes.

"Then one day when I got back from a trip," he told
us, "I found Mike, David, and Flo sitting in a happy huddle
around the remains of my camp bed. As I walked up they ambled away with the last few shreds of canvas, leaving me with
the twisted metal frame!" After that, Kris locked things up,
and for a few days the chimps hunted there in vain.

"The end of it all was beautiful," Kris said with a grin.
"I was sitting writing notes when Flo walked past. She peered
round, looking for something to steal, but everything was hidden. Then she spied my cigarette lighter in a red cloth case
on the table. She gave a squeak of delight, grabbed it, and
hurried off with her trophy!"

Luckily for Kris, the chimps did not fancy his precious
plant presses, particularly as they were sprayed with insecti-
cide. But the safety of our own notes, our files and files of
notes, caused us constant worry. Indeed, Edna just managed
to save one file Mr. McGregor had stolen. They both pulled
and, although Edna hung on to the contents, Mr. McGregor
got away with most of the cover.

None of the precious scientific material was lost, however, and by the end of 1964 the record was large and impressive. We not only kept detailed notes of each day's happenings,
but also a file for every individual chimp in which we entered
the salient points of his behavior. We drew charts to help keep
at least some of the vast quantity of data in a form we could
refer to quickly, to check on various aspects of behavior.

Over and above this paper work, Hugo had already
recorded a fairly comprehensive selection of chimpanzee calls
on tape and had begun to build up an outstanding scientific
film record of chimpanzee behavior, thanks to a grant from
the National Geographic Society.

Hooting apes stage frenzied rain dances when pelted by a downpour. In this sequence a chimpanzee first crouches, then stands erect and plunges down a slope, yelling all the while. Grabbing a branch, he slaps the ground as he charges toward a tree, and climbs the trunk. Hurling himself downward, he snaps off a bough and drags it behind him. To break his headlong rush he swings around a tree. Finally, he plods uphill to turn and charge again. Mothers and their young watch from the ridge.

Wet and dejected, 12-year-old Pepe sits hunched after a rainstorm; he yawns in frustration and spins streaks of water from his glistening black coat. Annoyed by drops trickling down their bodies, chimps often pick handfuls of leaves to rub themselves dry. Straight, coarse hair protects them against getting soaked to the skin—except in a deluge.

"Bulbous nose, drooping lower lip, well over 35 to put it mildly," Jane says of Flo.

Four apes in a huddle attest the animals' preference for traveling in small bands; females and their young form the only stable groups. Here, Flo rubs an itchy nose as young Gigi crowds between her and Goliath, who held the top rank among the Gombe Stream chimps when the author named him. At that time Mike (left) was one of the lowliest of the apes.

Out of character, short-tempered J. B. (left) places an affable hand on Fifi's head. In an intense gesture of greeting at right, Rodolf rhythmically clacks his teeth and grooms Mike's shoulder.

*Raging current endangers newlyweds Jane and Hugo as they
flee torrential rains that forced them to abandon an effort
to drive 840 miles from Nairobi to Kigoma, near the reserve.
In their retreat the two barely escaped being trapped between
flooded rivers. By backtracking more than 100 miles and
boarding a train, they finally reached their destination.*

90

David gorges himself on fruit while Fifi watches imploringly; when on a binge the big male can eat 60 bananas, one after another. At right, David bends a twig to snack on tiny seeds. Fifi (opposite, above) nibbles leaves. Chimps spend about seven hours a day feeding. Yawning widely, Rodolf shows teeth worn with chewing; cavities may well cause bad temper in some chimps. Apes, like humans, grow only one set of permanent teeth. Rubbery-jawed Pooch tries to remove the sticky white residue from a meal of milk-pod seeds.

Waiting hungrily, Flint and Flo beg gluttonous David Greybeard for a bite of baboon; each got a morsel — Flo part of the meat and her baby a bit of bone. High in a fig tree, Rodolf jealously guards his kill, occasionally allowing J. B. a taste. The author learned from her observations that the apes supplement their largely vegetarian diet with meat, apparently considering it a delicacy. Gombe Stream chimpanzees prey on monkeys and the young of bushbuck and bushpig.

Peering into a looking glass, young Evered sees himself for the first time—and his hair stands on end! Melissa, "feminine through and through," takes a front seat at right as two curious companions strain for a look. When old Flo saw herself, she screamed in fright.

Mouth crammed with food, David clings to a stolen blanket. The author instructs her assistants to let the animals take what they want—so they won't feel frustrated or angry. At left, Mike and J. B. stare at a stuffed toy; wary—like all wild chimps—of anything new, they refused to play with it. But later, young Fifi groomed the doll when her mother kept her from playing with her baby brother.

Indulging a taste for glue, apes munch cardboard, then spit out the pulped pieces. Huge
Rodolf drapes his hands over the box above
while Flo fondles little Flint; orphaned Merlin
nibbles at the flap and sister Miff edges in closer.
At right, David Greybeard shares with Pooch.
"If a female whimpers," Jane says, "he'll tear
off a scrap of carton for her."

Juvenile delinquent: Adolescent Figan purloins a pillow. First he wrestled with it, then somersaulted on it, and finally ended in a cloud of feathers when the cloth ripped. The chimp clung to the tattered fabric through the night and played with it all the following day.

*At day's end the husband-wife
team and assistant Edna Koning relax
in the glow of a campfire
as they listen to taped screams, hoots,
and grunts—the sounds
of chimpanzees in the wild.*

David and Goliath
embrace in a palm tree,
overwhelmed by emotion at the
sight of a full stem of bananas.
Hugo holds the fruit aloft
to lure them to a new
chimp observation area.

4

The Way We Live and Work

WAVING HIS ARMS excitedly and speaking rapidly in Swahili, Hassan exclaimed, *"Davidi aliona mashua ya ndizi!"* – "David saw the boatload of bananas!" I can still hear his laughter as he told the story. David Greybeard, while quietly chewing on a stolen tea towel at the Africans' quarters near the lake, had spied Hassan bringing in our little boat with a load of bananas for the feeding area.

With grunts of delight, the hungry ape rushed toward the shore. Just in time Hassan pushed away from land and escaped with his tempting cargo. David stopped short at the water's edge, for the chimpanzees dislike getting their feet wet. Tossing the chimp an armload of the fruit to appease him, Hassan took the boat around a bend of the shore. There he waited while David consumed at least 40 bananas before plodding up the beach and into the forest.

We buy our bananas at Mwamgongo, a small fishing village just north of the reserve. One day Hugo and I decided to accompany Hassan to fetch the weekly supply. With us went Rashidi, a native of Mwamgongo, one of the Africans we employ to help with fetching, carrying, and distributing the fruit for the chimpanzee observation area at Main Camp.

As we approached the village by boat, we stared aghast. The mountains rose bare before us, devastated by the cutting of the forests, the farmers' annual burning of the ground cover, and the resultant erosion. The lush green woods I had grown to love did not extend beyond the boundary of the government reserve. Except for groves of mangoes and oil

palms planted in the valley, the only trees we could see were those straggling along the watercourses.

In years past, fishermen living along the shore had deforested the slopes. They cut vast numbers of trees not only for the building of huts and dugout canoes, but also for use in night fishing on Lake Tanganyika. For generations the Africans kindled wood fires in braziers on their fishing craft to create sufficient light to lure schools of sardine-size *dagaa* toward their nets.

"This valley must have been beautiful once, though," Hugo said as he gazed at the red, gullied earth.

Indeed, it must have been one of the loveliest of them all. The mountains tower some 3,000 feet above the lake, set back from the shore in a wide and almost perfect semicircle. The planted palm trees hide much of the village on the valley floor, but clusters of huts and single houses freckle the bare slopes above, almost to the topmost peaks.

On the flat beach thousands of dagaa lay drying in the morning sun. The fishermen worked among their catch of the night before, each moving slowly through his portion, prodding and flicking the fish over methodically with a long pole so they would dry evenly.

Four small, naked boys with toy sailing canoes splashed about in the shallows at the edge of the lake. As they saw us they ducked down into the water with exaggerated yells of hastily assumed modesty. Pushing their homemade sailboats through the blue-green ripples, they glanced toward us repeatedly with mischievous grins.

Walking or loping on all fours, chimps travel with a slightly sidling step, occasionally freeing one arm to carry objects or to drag a branch; infants sometimes ride like diminutive jockeys. The nomadic apes wander as far as ten miles a day in quest of food.

By the time we reached shore a small crowd had gathered, and many willing hands helped us beach the boat. Hugo and I set out to explore the village, leaving Hassan to supervise the loading of the bananas brought from neighboring plantations in anticipation of our arrival.

With Rashidi as guide, we walked along paths shaded by giant mangoes. Everywhere among the trees and houses lay patches of neatly planted *muhogo,* or cassava. Villagers grind the root into a white flour used in mixing a paste called *ugali.* Dipped in sauces made from dagaa, Nile perch, tilapia, or, occasionally, chicken, the thick lumps of ugali make up the staple food for the settlement.

Along the way, Rashidi pointed out several buildings constructed of stone, with grass-covered metal roofs. In these, he informed us, lived the notables of Mwamgongo. However, most of the dwellings were of sun-baked earthen bricks, with thatch roofs.

HUGO FOUND he needed cigarettes, so we visited one of the two village dukas. Once inside, we gazed in amazement at the variety of merchandise. The small store held dishes and shoes, soap and sugar—even a huge string bag filled with brown rubber balls for children.

Proudly, Rashidi showed us the school—a long, low building of three rooms. We arrived after class, held from eight in the morning until noon. On one wall hung a huge, neatly drawn diagram of the human eye. A blackboard displayed simple words chalked in Swahili, the language the schoolchildren learn in addition to their local tongue. In fact, Swahili and English serve as the official languages of Tanzania. Outside, we crossed a flat, open space. "*Futiboli,*" said Rashidi, encompassing with a sweep of his arm the deserted patch of bare ground and the somewhat lopsided goalposts of the soccer field.

We visited Rashidi's home, and Hugo took pictures of the family. But he had no luck in photographing other aspects of village life. One handsome young girl sat shelling beans outside her hut, surrounded by small children and a collection of large pottery cooking vessels.

"Ask if it will be all right if I take her picture," Hugo said to Rashidi in Swahili.

Rashidi approached her, and we saw her flash a coy smile as she began to speak liltingly in Kiha, the language of a local Bantu tribe called the Waha.

"She says yes, it's all right—but she wants money for posing," Rashidi translated.

Crutch gait, or "swing walk," speeds a chimp downhill. Beginning on all fours, the ape lifts his weight on long, powerful arms and propels his legs forward, then crouches again to repeat the motion.

"O.K. How much?" As a rule we gave out no more than four or five shillings for a picture.

"*Shilingi ishirini*"—"20 shillings"—said the girl, who then broke into giggles behind her hand, a signal for everyone to join in the joke! By local standards, these villagers are quite prosperous. They raise cassava as a cash crop, and sell their catches of dagaa in Kigoma as food for laborers on sisal plantations and in copper mines to the south. They do not feel the need for money, nor do they really care to have their pictures taken.

BEFORE CLIMBING into the boat, now loaded high with bananas for the return trip, we paused to watch a group of men planking a canoe. Today one rarely sees the old dugout, hollowed from a tree trunk. The Africans prefer modern flat-bottomed canoes because they are larger, more stable in the water, and better suited to fishing.

Once back at the reserve, we quickly put the bananas into temporary storage in two strongly built huts on the lakefront. The staff always waits until late evening to carry the fruit to the store near the Main Observation Camp, covering each load with layers of sacking to camouflage it from any late-wandering chimpanzee. Two sets of doors on the main storeroom enable us to enter without exposing the bananas to view. It would be disastrous indeed if one of the adult male chimps ever glimpsed the golden treasure hanging inside.

Our African staff works hardest at dusk. Rashidi and Ramadhani, another employee of ours, cope with the bananas. They clear out the concrete boxes, carry away peelings discarded by the chimps during the day—if we leave the skins, they attract baboons to the feeding area—and refill the boxes with bananas for the next day. Invariably, a broken wire or a dislodged pipe needs repair.

Meanwhile Anyango and Ramadhani's younger brother, Sadiki, fetch water from the stream 300 yards away, light lamps, sweep and tidy the rooms, and wash the day's dishes. Another cook, Benjamin, who accompanies Hugo and me on wildlife studies in the Serengeti National Park, helps Anyango with the housework and cooking when we are at the reserve.

The day that Hugo's half brother Michael arrived, he asked how we ran the camp and the research. We explained as best we could.

With manlike posture and a waddling step, chimpanzees often walk erect across open ground. When leaping, the apes bound as far as six feet from a standing start.

"But don't they get bored, your staff?" Michael asked. "I mean, not having anything to do all day."

I smiled. "Why don't we go down to the beach and show Michael," I suggested to Hugo.

We got there about 11 o'clock and found the Africans' camp buzzing with activity. Hassan sat outside his tent with hammer and nails, transforming a packing case into a cupboard. Since joining us at the reserve, he has made much of our furniture from whatever scraps of wood were available.

Nearby, Rashidi and Ramadhani swept one of the banana storerooms. The last few overripe bananas went to the ducks and chickens that ran about.

At lakeside, one of Rashidi's sons proudly cleaned our new boat, furnished us by the National Geographic Society. Surprisingly roomy, the 16-foot fiberglass Boston Whaler carries an impressive amount of equipment and supplies with ample room left over to seat four adults comfortably. The sturdy little craft skims the waters of Lake Tanganyika at speeds of 20 knots and more.

Hassan can now make the 16-mile trip to Kigoma for mail and provisions in 40 minutes or so, as contrasted with the two and a half to three hours required in the old boat. On his periodic trips, he frequently overtakes the lake's public "water taxis," loaded to capacity with cargo and passengers. It takes only minutes to leave them far astern.

Michael, who had stood idly watching the cleaning of the boat, looked up and saw Anyango bustling about in the kitchen—a simple open-sided hut with a grass roof. We explained that he was making bread.

"When the dough rises," I told Michael, "Anyango puts it under a *karai*—one of those huge metal bowls over there. Then he heaps glowing charcoal over the karai so that it becomes an oven."

"It certainly makes jolly good crispy bread," said Michael, who had been visibly impressed at breakfast. "Not like the doughy stuff you get in England."

Outside Sadiki's little house, his wife carefully smoothed and plaited her daughter's hair, using a hand-carved wooden comb. Some of the local coiffures, amazingly elaborate, look rather like imaginative patterns one might find carved on the heads of wooden idols.

Nearby, two small boys, each wearing a grubby waist-length vest, played with an ingenious toy consisting of a long stick with a shorter crosspiece lashed to one end. The youngsters had used knives to hollow out two *Strychnos* fruits and had attached one to each end of the shorter stick. When they pushed the toy, the round fruits revolved like wheels.

Next Michael noticed the charcoal hand iron—a most useful gadget that enables us to look neat and tidy in the bush. Benjamin stood filling it with red-hot charcoal pilfered from Anyango's bread oven.

FARTHER ALONG the beach, Ramadhani's beautiful wife took her turn at drying a square of fish her husband had helped catch—members of our staff often go out with the fishermen. Her five-year-old daughter worked with her own tiny turning stick. Beyond them, silhouetted against the brilliant blue of the lake, Sadiki did our washing.

"Well, you can't say they look bored, any of them, can you?" I said to Michael. He agreed, but looked puzzled as he gazed around the Africans' camp.

"I thought you had a cook called Dominic?" he said. "I read about him in your GEOGRAPHIC articles."

We explained that Dominic had left the reserve. After saving a good bit of money while working with us, he had built a house in Kigoma and gone to live there with his wife, child, and aged father. His leaving had saddened us, for he had been with the staff since that July day in 1960 when my mother and I first stepped ashore at the reserve, equipped with only the barest kitchen essentials.

I have always felt that Dominic was secretly shocked when he discovered that our tableware consisted of a thermos top, a cup with a broken handle, and a couple of tin plates. With his skill as a cook and with his delightful personality, he had soon become a valued companion as well as a great help to my mother and me.

Michael then saw ten-year-old Petro, son of one of the fishermen, hurrying toward us along the beach. "What in the world has he got?" he asked, noticing that the boy carried a jam jar in one outthrust hand.

"*Dudu,*" Petro said breathlessly, holding the jar out to Hugo for his inspection.

"That's Swahili for insect," I told Michael. "Hugo gives one shilling for any that he wants to film."

This time Petro had captured a truly spectacular prize, a praying mantis that looked like an ideal subject for photographic study. The jar speedily changed hands to the mutual satisfaction of Hugo and Petro. The boy set off at a run toward the forest, undoubtedly to continue his hunting.

"Petro usually helps us hand out medicine to the fishermen," I told Michael. "We do that twice a week and he loves to act as orderly for our clinic. You know, to count out pills, cut off strips of bandage, and things."

My mother started this medical service not long after we arrived at the reserve. In the beginning, she had requests for simple things such as aspirin, cough syrup, and adhesive tape. Then one day a really sick patient named Kondo arrived, supported by two friends.

Examining him, my mother found that an ulcer, probably the result of an infected scratch or insect bite, had eaten into the flesh of his ankle, exposing the bone. He refused to go to the hospital in Kigoma because one of his friends had just died there. So my mother tried an age-old remedy: the saline drip. Three times a day she cleansed the infected area with a simple solution of salt and lukewarm water. After a month her patient could walk with a stick and a few weeks later he seemed cured.

Word traveled quickly, for Kondo told his friends about the good woman doctor. Patients flocked in from the neighboring fishing villages, some of them walking as far as ten miles to get medical care. My mother soon found herself running a regular clinic. The fishermen appreciate the service we provide, and by and large it makes our relations with them very cordial indeed.

I shall never forget my initiation into my mother's medical venture. We had gone to bed one night when we heard Dominic's urgent voice from the darkness. "Very sick woman. Want you come quick," he said.

Dragging on some clothes, we followed him along the winding path, over the stream, to the hut of Iddi Matata. He greeted us, and led us through a smoke-filled central room where men and women chatted and laughed, and then into a second, smaller room. There we saw an African girl lying on the earth floor in the throes of childbirth. Her face felt cold as ice. Fearing that something had gone wrong, I ran back for hot tea and brandy. Then my mother and I helped with the delivery as best we could.

Finally the baby, a girl, was born. Old Iddi, with great ceremony, cut the umbilical cord with a pair of scissors which, he told us proudly, he kept especially for just such a purpose. On that memorable night, there in the dimly lit hut, I saw for the first time the miracle of human birth. The mother was young and the baby her first. Despite the ordeal she had endured, her eyes reflected wonder as she gazed down at the tiny masterpiece of nature in her arms.

DECEMBER, 1964, saw the beginning of one of the major changes at the reserve—we started work on our new buildings for the Main Observation Camp. We had requested funds for them from the National Geographic Society because life under canvas had become increasingly unbearable. The chimpanzees not only stole our clothing, blankets, cardboard, and paper, but during their wild charging displays they also pulled out guy ropes, broke tent poles, dragged tables and chairs, and hurled any small pieces of equipment that they could lay hands on.

We selected a spot that offered a superb view of the surrounding mountains. Once more we moved at night, because the only path to the new site led through the Ridge Camp observation area, and we were anxious to disturb the chimpanzees as little as possible.

Headman Iddi Matata cuts the umbilical cord of an African baby the author and her mother helped deliver. Smiling broadly, the father holds a lantern.

For our buildings we had chosen light, prefabricated aluminum to ease the job of carrying everything in darkness across a mile of treacherous, hilly ground. Even the erection of these simple structures involved a great deal of hard work, both for the Africans we employed and for Hugo, who supervised the project.

To prepare the concrete foundations for the new Main Observation Camp, the men dug great chunks out of the rocky mountainside. Our house to this day has a large rock jutting from the floor—for without a bulldozer we could not change the site we had mapped out, and without explosives we could not dislodge the obstruction. Sand and gravel, as well as cement and the sections of the buildings themselves, had to be carried up from the beach. Hugo estimated that in completing the work the porters walked a total of 2,000 miles.

Every evening after supper Hugo climbed to the clearing to make sure the work was progressing satisfactorily, to check on the number of loads carried by each person, and to see that the site was level and the concrete mixed in the right proportions. Sometimes, my own tasks finished, I joined him at the new location.

When I did, it seemed strange — first the walk through the familiar valley, dark and full of the nighttime mystery that I had come to know and love, and then the faint glow of light through the trees and the unaccustomed sounds, growing louder as I approached, of the talk and laughter of the working men. The slow but steady advance of the program both excited and saddened me because it meant not only progress but also the end of the old days.

From the new site we can see the lights of the African fishing canoes on Lake Tanganyika, looking like so many fireflies hovering just above the water. Kerosene pressure lamps have long since replaced the wood-fire braziers on the boats. Now each craft carries one or two of the lamps fixed securely to a wooden platform at the bow, and each is crewed by two Africans. One of the fishermen sits in the stern and paddles slowly to keep the canoe on a straight course; the other, armed with a long-handled, rust-colored net, stands near the pressure lamps, ready to scoop up the dagaa when they swim to the surface.

This method of fishing is limited to two weeks or so a month, for when the moon is out the lamps are not bright enough to attract the dagaa. At such times the fishermen leave the reserve, where they have permission to set up temporary camps during the dry season only, to sell or take to their families their sun-dried catch.

On dark nights, however, we can usually see some 80 lights bobbing on the lake. Often, apparently to make the fish jump, the oarsmen sing loudly and bang their paddles against the sides of the canoes, while the men with the nets stamp their feet in time to the rhythm. Sometimes, late at night, the lake reverberates with a din that sounds like the climax of a boisterous party.

THE CONSTRUCTION WORK at the Main Observation Camp continued for nearly three months. Finally, two days before Hugo and I had to leave, the buildings were up — a single room for Hugo and me, a larger structure with a work room, a small kitchen, and two bedrooms for the girls, and not far away a storeroom for bananas.

Concrete feeding boxes stocked with bananas awaited

Gombe Stream specialty, tilapia ste
simmers over blazing logs. Anyango, the camp coo
finds the tasty fish ready to ser

the chimps, and we again faced the problem of introducing them to another location. We decided to string bananas along the path toward the camp, and lead some of the chimps to the start of the trail. The distance was too great for a repetition of Hugo's previous escapade with the empty box.

The plan, however, never materialized. When Hugo and I reached the buildings, we noticed David and Goliath feeding in a palm tree on the far side of the valley. Nothing could have been better. We quickly took a stalk of ripe bananas from the store and held it aloft.

Neither of the apes had seen such an abundance of the fruit for some time. They stared in our direction for a full ten seconds without reacting, as though they could not accept the evidence of their eyes. Then with piercing screams they embraced, each pressing his mouth to the other's body in the typical way of highly excited chimps. For at least a minute they remained in the tree. Then, still screaming in excitement, they swung down and hurried across the valley toward us.

B Y THIS TIME the bedlam had attracted every chimpanzee in the vicinity. We heard wild yells converging from all over the valley. Soon the first of the mob appeared on the steep path, calling hysterically. We scattered bananas liberally on the ground but the chimps, although they gathered them up, seemed too emotional to eat. Instead, they continued to embrace, pat, and kiss.

When they finally calmed down a bit, they began to feed. The mouthfuls of fruit gradually muffled their cries. By the time Hugo and I were ready to leave the reserve, nearly all the chimps we knew had discovered the feeding area at the Main Observation Camp with no effort on our part. Edna and Sonia moved their belongings from Ridge Camp and installed themselves in the sturdy new buildings.

Now the time had come for me to return to Cambridge University and for Hugo to begin his work of editing the film for the National Geographic Society. We were, as always, saddened at the thought of going, but at least we had no worry about our assistants. The two girls could lock their belongings and our irreplaceable records — and themselves if necessary — into the buildings. And, most important, they could continue making observations and keeping data at the reserve until Hugo and I returned the following year.

Wearing *kanga* cloth from Holla▮

Bearded Iddi Matata, who acts as honorary headman at the reserve, welcomed Jane when she arrived in 1960. He still lives there among his children and grandchildren, and greets visitors at Kasekera. But other members of the Gombe community have moved away. Dominic has taken his wife Chiko (opposite) and his daughter Ado to live in Kigoma. Outside the family's tent at the author's first camp, Ado gets her hair styled by her mother, who uses a hand-carved wooden comb. Dominic still helps Jane and Hugo on occasion: He sent his friend Prosper (opposite), an immigrant from the Congo, to help mix concrete for the permanent buildings at the Main Observation Camp.

...omen of the Ha tribe gossip and bargain over fresh fruit at the market on Kigoma's main street.

Dense forest cloaks the Kakombe Stream valley above Lake Tanganyika. Open woodland of the steep upper slopes makes the region ideal for chimp-watching. New aluminum buildings house Jane's African staff; thatched huts of Game Scouts and fishermen line the beach.

Silvery catch of *dagaa* carpets the lakeshore near a fishing hut. Long-poled nets take their color from a dye made of the red clay of termite mounds. To cook the fish Africans dip them in ground cassava root and fry them in palm oil. At left, Dominic fills a sack for market.

Youthful Ha tribesman flutes an *mwirunge,* an instrument fashioned from a length of bamboo.

Scientist admires a toy dugout at Mwamgongo, a fishing village north of the reserve. White-sandaled Rashidi, who assists Jane at the camp, explains how his son carved the boats for children to sail on Lake Tanganyika. The freshwater lake, one of the world's largest, stretches 420 miles down a valley of the Great Rift, and at its deepest plunges 4,710 feet.

Nimble fingers flip seeds from cup to cup in a game of *bao.* Seemingly illogical moves often baffle outsiders who try to master the rules.

Haystack on stilts serves as a wilderness kitchen and bakery for the author and her staff.

Barefoot Dominic hoes a forest garden. He attempted to grow tomatoes and cucumbers for the camp staff, but pigs and baboons raided the plot and ate the tender shoots. Long fishing rods lean against a platform raised to keep camp utensils above the heads of roaming animals. Squatting at left, an assistant binds bamboo poles to make a fence. Later, jostling chimps knocked it down. Over a tiny flame, a fisherman's wife (opposite, above) roasts *sangara* taken from Lake Tanganyika. Dominic's wife tends a smoky fire as she stews the fish in palm oil.

Dispensing aspirin, Epsom salts, and adhesive tape, the author's mother, Mrs. Vanne Morris-Goodall, oversees the camp clinic she set up in 1960. Below, she treats children from neighboring settlements to pieces of hard candy.

Speaking Swahili, Jane gives encouragement — and milk of magnesia — to a Bantu boy. Africans living in villages around the reserve occupy one of the most remote parts of Tanzania. Many have walked as far as ten miles to obtain medicine at the camp. One young mother, feverish with malaria, carried her son six miles to the wilderness clinic.

Sun's fading splendor silhouettes fishing
canoes off the shore of the reserve
as Africans prepare for a night of dagaa
· fishing. At full dark, bright pressure
lamps lure the tiny fish toward the nets.

Hair bristling, Pepe drums his chest like a gorilla — a charging display rare among chimps. Other males watch from the shade of a palm.

5

David Greybeard and His World

HOW BETTER CAN I DESCRIBE the everyday activities of the chimpanzees than to tell of a day in the life of my old friend David Greybeard? David — the first chimpanzee to accept me completely, the first to allow me quite near him. What a triumph that had been! I had come upon him unexpectedly, and when he saw me, he merely stared for a moment, then casually continued munching grass. That was in 1961, when I had been in the field just over a year. The day I shall now detail occurred in June of 1966.

The alarm clock rang as usual at 5:30 a.m. I dressed by moonlight, ate a quick breakfast, and headed for my rendezvous with David Greybeard. The night before, I had seen him making a nest in a miombo tree, and now I hurried through the ghostly forest to a place where I could see him in his nest. Once there, I settled down to wait for dawn.

Gazing at the dark shapes of the trees in the pale light, I thought back over the years I had known David and observed his wanderings. I remembered too the many times I had watched chimpanzees in their nests. While they slept in comfort on springy beds, anywhere from 15 feet to 80 feet above the ground, I dozed fitfully while balanced precariously in a tree or on some steep mountain slope. But no matter how uncomfortable my situation, I delighted in the long nights I spent in the mountains.

A slight rustle from David's nest drew my attention. I realized that the first light of dawn had crept over the eastern mountains. David lazily scratched himself and yawned widely.

For ten minutes after sitting up he groomed himself and yawned repeatedly, as though loath to leave his comfortable bed. He had slept as mature males often do, alone and out of sight of other chimpanzees. Finally he decided it was time to begin the day. He climbed to the ground, gazed around as if wondering where to go, then plodded up the valley.

I followed, keeping about ten yards behind. When we reached a stream David paused for a drink before jumping across. Soon he stopped to eat sprays of berries, and I ate a few of them too. They tasted sweet, rather than sour or astringent like many of the chimpanzees' foods. As I looked at David's familiar, placid figure, I found it hard to believe that recently the same chimp, screaming in fury, had chased Hugo and me up a mountainside.

That chilling incident occurred while the chimps were eating a red colobus monkey they had captured in the Kakombe Stream valley. In trying to get close enough to see through the undergrowth, Hugo and I had approached too silently. The apes were startled when they saw us, and the males in the group, already worked up by their struggle to get shares of meat, rushed us, waving their arms and uttering savage calls. We stood our ground, thinking it all a bluff, until David, leaving the others, continued his charge.

At the last moment, we turned and fled. It was like a nightmare. Every time we looked back he seemed even closer. And Hugo, who stayed behind me and kept turning to face David, became trapped in a tangle of thorns. Helplessly he watched the screaming ape bear down upon him across

Cape buffalo stampede
within yards of the author.
Deceptively placid, the
beasts possess such
great strength and
ferocity that only
lions dare attack them.

the few yards that separated them. Suddenly, when it seemed he must attack, David stopped. For a moment he stood quite still, staring at each of us in turn; then he turned away and rejoined the noisy group gathered around the kill. Recovering our composure, we picked up the belongings we had dropped during our flight and returned to observe the chimpanzees from a more discreet distance.

David, normally so peaceful, is nonetheless the chimp we fear most. The other mature males, though they threaten us, seem somehow to be held back from actual attack, and we make a point of facing up to them. But David is different and although he might have been bluffing when he charged us we would have been foolish to wait and find out.

THERE WAS NOTHING FIERCE about David now. Having eaten his fill of berries, he climbed a steep slope and vanished into thick undergrowth, an easy enough path for a chimp walking on all fours but difficult for me. At one point I thought I had lost him, but shortly I saw that he had climbed a tree and begun eating leaf buds. With low-pitched grunts of pleasure, he bent the branches toward him with one hand and picked off the food with his lips.

As I watched my old friend, I thought back to a close encounter with wild animals in almost this same spot. I had followed Flo, Fifi, and Figan through the dim, vine-tangled forest. Suddenly, the chimps stopped and became quite still, watching and listening; after a moment, they walked on, moving silently over the damp leaves. I followed, curious about what they had heard. Again they paused and Figan, standing erect and peering about, gave the soft "hoo" of an anxious chimp. Fifi climbed a small tree, her hair bristling slightly.

Then I too heard a sound. A stick cracked as though a heavy animal had trodden on it. I tried to look through the heavy growth of lianas, but although the noise had seemed less than 20 yards away I could see nothing. Then with startling suddenness the forest resounded with the thunder of crashing bodies, snapping branches, and thudding hooves — buffalo! My scent must have stampeded the herd.

When the great beasts quieted, I stealthily climbed a tree and caught sight of two of them. Except for a constant switching of their tails they stood motionless. Twice more the buffalo milled wildly before moving away. The chimps, after taking to the trees during the first stampede, descended and to my surprise settled down calmly to rest. But even though they seemed unperturbed, it was quite a while before *my* heart stopped thumping.

An abrupt movement turned my thoughts again to David. He had been sitting quietly feeding in the tree for about an hour. Now he clambered down and once again set off up the mountainside, heading this time toward the Peak, on my old path. How many times, I wondered as I followed, had I tramped this trail, slipping and skidding on a dry burnt surface or squishing through tall drenched grass? How many times had I sped down it in the evening, trying to make the descent before the last golden flush of sunset left the mountain in darkness? I knew every turn, recognized almost every tree.

Without warning, David stopped and his hair began to rise. Standing erect, he peered along the path for a moment, then hurried forward on all fours. I hastened after him and saw the reason for his behavior — another male chimpanzee ran toward him through the grass. As the two drew closer they stood upright and swaggered slightly from foot to foot. Then they embraced and each pressed his mouth against the other's neck. With happy grunts they began grooming, their movements rapid and frenzied. The newcomer was Goliath, still one of David's most frequent companions.

Obviously delighted at meeting, the two great males swung into a tree after the initial excitement was over and settled down on a wide branch for a long period of grooming. Each parted the hair of his companion, closely examined the exposed skin, and picked off with fingers or lips small flakes of dried skin, grass seed, or the occasional tick picked up from vegetation. Contrary to popular belief, the two were not "defleaing" each other — the wild chimpanzee has no fleas. Grooming of this sort, one of the major social activities of the chimpanzee community, serves a useful purpose as well as giving the apes pleasure. I guessed that the two would carry on their session for at least an hour and I decided to climb the Peak, which rose invitingly above me, and watch them from there.

S OON AFTER DISCOVERING the Peak those many months ago, I had carried up a small metal trunk. In it I kept a blanket, a flashlight, a few cans of food, and a jar of coffee so I could remain in the mountains at night. At the start of the rains that year, I had a grass hut built to protect the trunk from the weather.

Now I found that the hut had burned during a brush fire and the trunk had disappeared. My kettle, though, still hung from its rusty chain, the lid gone and a thick layer of dried green scum inside. Nearby lay two blackened cans I had used in previous years for heating soup.

From the Peak I can look out over the beautiful Kakombe Stream and Mlinda valleys. That day I chose a spot with a view of the Kakombe. My eyes caught the familiar gleam of a waterfall through the trees and on the opposite slope I saw a new landmark — a great red scar caused by a landslide during the previous rains.

Far up the valley I spotted a troop of red colobus monkeys. The treetops swayed and bounced as the acrobats made spectacular leaps from one tree to the next. High overhead a fan-tailed bateleur eagle circled with wings motionless. Now and then the mournful cry of a trumpeter hornbill floated across the valley, sounding like the wail of a fretful child.

Presently, from the top of the opposite ridge, came the sound of calling chimpanzees. I glanced at David and Goliath below me and saw them pause in their grooming to give answering hoots. About 20 minutes later a bedlam of hooting and screaming rose from the valley, much closer this time. David and Goliath, their hair on end, and calling loudly, dropped from the tree. As they crossed the open ridge below me, hurrying to join the excited group in the valley, they broke into a run, slapping the ground and stamping before they leaped up at a tree trunk to drum on it with their feet.

Quickly I trained my binoculars on the group below and almost at once I saw Pepe charging, beating his chest like a gorilla—a remarkable form of display I have rarely observed among the chimpanzees. I also saw the reason for all the uproar. For one thing, the apes were climbing into a tree laden with ripe fruit; when a large number of chimpanzees find such a tree they invariably swing rapidly from branch to branch, calling loudly until each finds a feeding place. To add to their excitement, a sexually attractive female was traveling with the group.

A retinue of six mature males courted her in turn. One by one they swung through the tree with exaggerated and stylized bounds and leaps before the final stage of the courtship, when they swayed and swaggered before her. Chimpanzees are promiscuous, and each mated with her. Then they calmly settled down to feed.

In the wild, these apes mate most frequently during moments of social excitement—such as the arrival at a feeding place or the meeting of two groups. As things quieted down, I watched the rest of the group, several females and youngsters, climb into the food tree. Among them I saw old Flo and recalled the time in 1963 when she had been sexually attractive too. Despite her decrepit appearance she had more suitors than any other female we have observed. The sexual attraction of the female normally lasts about ten days, but Flo's persisted almost five weeks. During that time, most of the males we know were her constant escorts.

For the first few days three-year-old Fifi tried to push suitors away from her mother but after that she seemed to accept the new state of affairs. Since then we have seen other youngsters behave in the same way, sometimes running to "protect" females other than their own mothers.

BELOW THE TREE, sudden hooting announced the arrival of David and Goliath. The group feeding in the branches looked down and hooted in response. For a short while, pandemonium broke out again as the newcomers swung into the tree and raced toward the sought-after female. Then, one after the other, they hurried to greet the top-ranking Mike. Goliath crouched submissively, pressing his lips to Mike's neck. David touched him on the back and groomed him for

Tree-dwelling red colobus monkeys feed on leaves and shoots, rarely descending to the ground. Though agile and swift, they fall prey to the meat-eating chimp.

a few moments. Their obeisance completed, the two moved away to find feeding places.

As David moved out along a branch, he passed one of the mothers, and she turned her rump toward him in submissive greeting. He touched her, as chimp etiquette demands, then greeted her infant, patting it gently on the head while it looked up at him with big staring eyes.

When all the apes began feeding quietly again, I climbed down the slope to the group. When I reached the tree, a few of the chimpanzees glanced at me for a moment, but most of them scarcely interrupted the rhythm of their chewing at the approach of so harmless a fellow primate. How different from my experiences five years before!

Just above me fed two-year-old Flint, keeping close to Flo and pausing now and then to play with his sister Fifi. Flo's two older offspring, adolescent Figan and the young mature male Faben, also sat feeding in the tree. I suspected, however, that Faben was with the group because of the sexually attractive female, rather than because of his mother. Two years before he had moved around with his family a good deal, but now he accompanied them less and less.

For fully two hours the group fed on the astringent purple fruit. Soon after midday, singly and in groups, the chimpanzees climbed from the tree to rest in the shade. I moved in still nearer. David lay on his side, his eyes shut. Figan and Fifi sprawled on their backs, their eyes closed tight, and old Flo groomed her eldest son, Faben. The other adults either dozed or sat in pairs or small groups in grooming sessions. Flint, however, with all the energy typical of a human child, played with little Goblin, whose mother Melissa rested near Flo. The two chased after each other through the lianas that hung overhead. Occasionally they wrestled or engaged in a bout of rib-tickling while each dangled by one hand. At such times I heard distinctive panting grunts, the chimpanzee equivalent of human laughter.

As CHIMPS GROW OLDER they play less and less frequently; but, in the wild, even the mature individuals enjoy a romp from time to time. An adult male may roll on the ground during some game with an infant or a juvenile. And, even less frequently, the mature chimps play among themselves. The first time I observed this, David and Goliath lay stretched out after a meal of figs. Goliath looked at his friend, then reached out to him, and for a while the two toyed with each other's fingers. After a few moments they sat up, and Goliath leaned over and tickled David in the ribs and neck until David shook with spasms of chimpanzee laughter. When it seemed he could bear it no longer, he gave a loud yell, leaped up, and ran toward a clump of bushes. Goliath followed and chased him around and around until they both flung themselves to the ground in exhaustion.

As David slept soundly among his peaceful companions, the breeze dropped and even in the deep shade the heat grew oppressive. The only sounds were the murmuring of the stream and the incessant shrilling of cicadas.

Drowsily the afternoon wore on. The chimpanzees slept and groomed by turns. An adolescent female joined the group and gave a few soft, panting grunts in greeting, but the other chimps scarcely glanced at her. She sat beside one of the resting males and began to groom him. Goblin, who had tired of his games with Flint, played quietly near his mother, scratching at the soil and now and then tossing a palm nut and fetching it, or waving a leafy twig. Then he made himself a tiny nest on the ground, bending down small plants and sitting on each in turn.

About four o'clock, when the worst heat was over, David awoke, scratched himself in his deliberate way, and walked a few steps away from the others. Some of them looked up, but none of the adult males showed any inclination to go along—though there are times when just such behavior will initiate a concerted movement to a new feeding area.

David plodded away, and Flo, with Flint astride her back, got up and followed. Fifi quickly scampered after them. At the last moment, as though unable to make up his mind, nine-year-old Figan also hurried after his mother. I followed them to a stream and watched as they drank. Flint, filled with his mother's milk, was not thirsty. He crouched above a small pool and studied his reflection in the still water. Leaning down until his nose nearly touched the surface, he dabbed a finger at his mirrored face, then ran to jump onto Flo's back before she sprang to the opposite bank.

Once across the stream, the chimpanzees headed for Main Camp. As I looked up I saw Caroline and Sally moving about outside. David picked up speed as he realized that an evening meal of bananas waited just ahead.

Trailing the group toward camp, I recalled the hooting and grunting I had heard when David and Goliath joined the others earlier in the day, and I pondered the question of chimpanzee communication.

The apes have a large vocabulary of calls, each signifying an emotion such as fear, pain, or pleasure. When a group arrives at a food-laden tree and gives excited "food barks,"

Leaping apes bridge a mountain stream while one pauses for a drink. Finicky about their feet, the chimpanzees will swing through trees to avoid wading a rivulet.

other chimps within earshot often call in response and hurry to the feast. If one chimp gives a low, uneasy "hoo" when he sights an alarming object, others always peer in the same direction. When a youngster screams in fright or pain his mother invariably hurries to him.

T HE CHIMPANZEES have also evolved a complex nonverbal communication based on touch, posture, and gesture, in many respects almost identical to the nonverbal communication used by man. Gesture and facial expression play a major role among humans. For instance, an arm placed gently around another's shoulder may convey a message of sympathy more eloquently than words. The expression on a face can reveal the feelings of the speaker more surely than his voice. In fact, without the winking, smiling, nodding, raising of eyebrows, and shrugging of shoulders that go along with the spoken word, our own communication with our fellows would be drab and cold indeed.

Chimpanzees rely to a very great extent on communication by touch during their interactions. Physical contact seems to play a particularly vital role in the apes' emotional life, especially during infancy, when the mother's touch provides the youngster with its chief source of security. When Flint began his first independent explorations he always rushed back to Flo at the slightest hint of danger or distress.

As he grew older he sought her embrace less often, but was still quick to run to her side and touch or hold her hair, or have a quick "security" suckle. The human infant turns to the mother for comfort and security in much the same way. Usually he also learns to associate some of her reassuring qualities with other members of the family group, just as little Flint learned to run to his sister Fifi for comfort when Flo was not close by.

The apes' need for physical contact persists throughout life. When slightly anxious or worried, a chimpanzee usually reaches out to touch another. When emotionally disturbed to a greater extent, he often flings his arms around a companion. This embrace is probably the greatest form of reassurance an adult chimp can give or receive. On one occasion David Greybeard, threatened by a huge male baboon, ran screaming to fling his arms around Goliath and then, as if made brave by this contact with his friend, he ran toward the baboon and threatened it. Another time David became terrified by his reflection in a sheet of looking glass. He turned to four-year-old Fifi, who happened to be standing close by, and hugged her. Even contact with one so small seemed to comfort him, for his look of fear slowly lessened and after a moment he released Fifi and went to investigate the glass. Overexcited chimpanzees also embrace, as did David and Goliath when they saw the new supply of bananas at the buildings, and as did the three chimps when they watched Rodolf killing the young baboon.

The deep-seated need for reassuring physical contact shows very clearly when a chimp is threatened or attacked by a social superior. On such occasions he usually continues to scream and make submissive gestures until the aggressor calms him with a touch.

Once young Evered, set upon viciously by Goliath, fled in panic. A short distance away, however, he stopped and hesitantly walked back toward his attacker. He was still so frightened that he turned repeatedly as if to run away again. When at last his zigzag approach took him close enough, he crouched low to the ground and turned his rump to Goliath. He remained thus, screaming and looking back over his shoulder, until the big male reached out and patted him reassuringly, continuing for several moments until Evered's screams died away. Once Figan, threatened by pugnacious J. B., shrieked in fear and held his hand palm up toward his mother Flo. She responded by reaching out to hold her son's hand until his cries ceased.

The chimps' behavior often reminds me of that of people. I once watched a child who had been smacked for some naughtiness follow her mother from room to room, clutching at her skirt and crying until finally the mother relented. She comforted her daughter by kissing her and stroking her hair, and gradually the child's crying stopped. Often I have seen a youngster after a stern reprimand wait with trembling lips until the parent gave a few reassuring pats.

Some of our chimps go out of their way to ingratiate themselves with their superiors. Melissa, for instance, always hurries toward high-ranking males to lay her hand submissively on their backs, or to crouch low before them. And an adolescent male repeatedly pays his respects to a particular mature male — not necessarily the top-ranking adult.

By walkie-talkie, Jane tells her car
staff that she intends to stay overnight in t
mountains, observing chimps in their nes

Chimpanzees, like people, exchange greetings when they meet after being apart for any length of time. When this occurs, an observer can usually determine the relationship of one chimp to the other. They may meet as two friends and show pleasure in their reunion, or one may make submissive gestures, acknowledging the other's higher rank.

When Mike arrives in any group the other chimps invariably hurry to pay their respects, touching him with outstretched hands or bowing, just as courtiers once bowed before their king. And, just as the king chose either to acknowledge a courtier or to ignore him, so Mike may take notice of his inferiors, touching them briefly, or he may do nothing. Depending on his mood, he may even threaten or strike those who hasten to greet him.

Many of the apes' forms of greeting startlingly resemble our own. They often kiss. Rodolf in particular frequently touches the face of a subordinate with his lips, or presses his open mouth onto the neck or shoulder of another adult male. Pepe and Figan, to mention but two, often press their mouths to the lips of other individuals. Hand-holding, as a gesture of greeting, is not common in the chimpanzee community at the reserve, but it does occur. Melissa for one, when first arriving in a group, occasionally holds her hand toward a dominant male until he reaches out and reassures her with a touch.

O NE OF THE MOST MEMORABLE REUNIONS took place between old Mr. Worzle and timid Olly. As she approached him, panting nervously, he raised both arms as though pronouncing a blessing. Encouraged, Olly crept closer, crouching and holding her hand toward him. Mr. Worzle took her hand in his and drew her close, placing his other hand gently on her head. Then each flung both arms around the other and exchanged kisses on the neck. Finally, to complete the picture, Olly's daughter Gilka ran up and Mr. Worzle reached out and drew her into his embrace.

The similarity of many chimpanzee gestures and postures to those of man is to Hugo and me one of the most exciting aspects of our study. It thrills us quite as much as the discovery that wild apes make and use crude tools. For either the gestures used by both man and ape have evolved along closely parallel lines, or they have a common origin in some remote ancestor of both man and ape.

In mutual grooming sessions, chimps pick off seeds, burrs, specks of dirt, and, occasionally, a tick. Half a dozen or more apes may assemble at midday, but normally two or three tend each other. Adults indulge in this social custom for an hour or so daily. Mothers groom tiny infants for only a few seconds, with sessions getting longer as the youngsters grow older. At left, Mr. McGregor inspects Rodolf. Flo (right) pushes Fifi's head back for a look at her neck.

Don't interrupt me now! Without pausing in his grooming of Melissa, Figan places a restraining hand on infant Flint, who wriggles and pants with laughter during a romp with Goblin. Hoisting a foot and concentrating intently, adolescent Figan grooms the calf of his leg (opposite, below), and Mr. McGregor, drenched by a sudden rain, scratches his back against a rough-barked palm to rub water from his coat.

Pulling her hair, Figan tickles Jane — and she and assistant Edna Koning try to avoid tickling Hugo while they cut his hair. Below, Flint peeks into a tent at the author, who pats him gently through the canvas. "We used to play with some of the chimps," says Jane. "Now we no longer touch them. The older ones may weigh as much as 175 pounds and are so strong they could easily hurt us without intending to."

Roving baboons of the Gombe Reserve rest at midday. Like the apes, these large monkeys travel on the ground, searching in groups for food. At left, a mother with a five-month-old on her back stops to bite into a fig. Adult females (at right, above, and at far right) average half the weight of the males, and lack the two-inch canine teeth. Mouth agape, a big male bares his fangs in a threat display. Even a leopard will turn away from a troop when the fierce males defend it. Though chimps on occasion kill baboons for food, the groups usually ignore each other. Sometimes, however, the youngsters play together or the adult males engage in mock battles.

Feeding peacefully, Goliath finds an adult male baboon close by. Resentfully, he leaps upright in a spectacular threat. The baboon flinches, then at the height of the display turns away to flee. Below, a large adolescent chimpanzee drives an aggressive baboon away from a banana box. First the ape screams and swings his arms from side to side, then flails them up and down as his cries grow in intensity. The baboon stands his ground for a moment before retreating. "These battles," the author says, "are mostly bluff. Actually, the chimps seem a bit scared at such times."

Chimps come calling at Pan Palace, named for their genus *Pan*—and all work ceases. At right, Melissa arrives with Goblin, interrupting Jane at her task of compiling a "character book." Pooch (above) peers curiously through a door at the observation camp, and the author pauses in her writing while Flint just hangs around.

Chimps communicate by touch and gesture as well as by calls. Melissa (above) seeks reassurance from Humphrey, who frequently bullies females. "She's holding her first baby," Jane explains, "and she feels very apprehensive." At left, Melissa extends a hand in supplication to Faben, a husky 12-year-old. He reaches out, palm turned down, and gives a calming touch. At right, Figan and Miff greet with a kiss.

Top-ranking ape, Mike stages a clattering display with empty kerosene cans and a heavy steel box. Squatting beside the containers, he rocks from side to side, hooting loudly. Then, his excitement mounting, he stands and bangs the cans together before hurling them in front of him. Charging at breakneck speed, he keeps as many as three bounding and clanging along the uneven ground. The author believes this noisy charging display frightened the other apes and gave Mike his high position. When Jane began her work at the reserve in 1960, Mike was one of the lowliest of the chimps and mighty Goliath ruled supreme. But after Mike discovered his "status symbols" and began his clangorous charges, Goliath was among the first to hurry to him, panting and bowing in submission.

Taking a siesta, chimps nap among branches as high as 80 feet above the ground. At left Huxley bends and twists boughs into a springy day nest — a task that requires less than five minutes. Figan (below) sprawls sound asleep, one hand holding a branch. Fifi dozes on a limb that arches above baby Flint, Gilka, and Flo. "Though chimps change position in their sleep, I've never known one to fall," the author says. "Their nests are quite safe — I think I could sleep in one if I had to."

Flint rescues tiny Goblin, stranded while playing high in a tree. Unable to reach another branch, the infant whimpered in distress until his friend hurried to help.

6

Mothers
and Their Young

ONE EVENING IN 1964, young Melissa arrived in camp with her first baby. As she walked slowly and carefully down the slope toward us, she paused every few steps to sit and gaze at the tiny infant in her lap.

When she moved on again, she pressed the baby close to her belly with one hand. An adult male accompanied her, but Melissa, normally so eager to please her superiors, paid him little attention; and when he wandered out of camp she did not follow. Again and again she stared down at the tiny creature come so suddenly into her life, her whole attitude and expression one of utter bewilderment.

Melissa must have given birth that day, for the placenta was still attached to the umbilical cord and trailed along the ground as she walked. Once it tangled in the undergrowth, nearly jerking the infant from her arms. Perhaps because of her inexperience as a mother, she had neither broken off nor bitten through the cord.

When Melissa left camp I followed. Darkness was near when she finally climbed a miombo tree to build a nest. With one hand she bent down branches and with the other supported the baby, whom we later named Goblin. After she lay down I left her there to experience for the first time since her own infancy the sharing of her bed with another.

"I wonder how she feels about the baby," Edna said as we sat around the fire at supper. The question lay uppermost in everyone's mind, for Melissa's dazed expression had left a deep impression on us.

"Well, I'm glad she seems to know how to cope with it," I said. "Some chimps in captivity seem so confused by their firstborn that they refuse to go near them. At times the poor little things have to be brought up by humans."

"Why do you suppose that is?" asked Edna.

"Probably," I replied, "it's got something to do with the fact that captive females don't usually get a chance to watch other mothers with babies, let alone handle and play with small infants the way these wild youngsters do."

"In other words," Hugo added, "in captivity the baby itself is something new and strange. With Melissa, it is simply the surprise of suddenly having one of her own."

As the days passed, Melissa gradually lost her baffled look and settled into her role as a mother. We soon discovered that while she looked after her infant quite well she was not particularly considerate of him. When Goblin struggled in vain to reach her breast, or when he slipped from her lap, she often ignored his tiny whimpers for several minutes before hoisting him into a better position. When at seven months he took his first uncertain steps, she seldom helped by placing a supporting hand under his tummy, nor did she support his back in his first clumsy efforts at climbing small branches. Often she paid no attention when he pulled her hand to his body, begging her to tickle him.

In sharp contrast to Melissa's rather offhand treatment of her infant was that of another young mother, Mandy. In the most solicitous manner, she never moved without first looking at the baby, and often climbed upside down in a sloth-like position as though to make sure that the infant, little Jane, would not fall. She frequently caressed her offspring and kissed its tiny hands and feet.

Despite her care, Mandy lost Jane when she was three months old. One day as a large group hurried to the feeding area we heard agonized cries. When Mandy arrived I saw that one of the baby's arms dangled useless and broken, with most of the flesh torn away. Mandy seemed utterly at a loss. Every time she moved, the infant screamed in pain, her eyes dull and glazed with suffering. The distressed mother's only response was to hug her tighter, thus making her scream still more. Not once did she so much as examine the wound. Now and again Jane turned to the greatest comfort an infant knows—her mother's milk—but that could not ease her agony. My eyes filled with tears, for I could do nothing to help. Had I tried to take Jane, Mandy would have fled with her, and trapping them might have provoked trouble from the other chimps.

Two days later we saw Mandy in the mountains, her baby dead. She had placed the body beside her while she groomed a companion and then, gathering up the sad burden, pressed it to her breast and went into the undergrowth. Somewhere in the forest Mandy abandoned the corpse, for she no longer had it when she came into camp the next day. How Jane's dreadful injury occurred we shall never know.

F IFTEEN MONTHS LATER, soon after Hugo and I returned to the reserve in 1966, we had cause for celebration. Mandy gave birth to another female. We were immediately struck by the difference in her treatment of this second offspring. Instead of worrying over it, she seemed scarcely to bother about it. Nor did she need to, for the tiny being clung to her even when Mandy leaped through the trees. We began to wonder whether Mandy's seeming oversolicitude for her firstborn had perhaps been due to a fundamental weakness of the infant itself, a weakness which may well have contributed to Jane's terrible accident.

When Mandy arrived with her second infant, the mature males were intrigued; but as they hurried toward her trying to get a better view, their hair on end with excitement, Mandy ran off in terror. Frustrated in their curiosity, the males charged and dragged branches, shook saplings and hurled rocks, while poor Mandy dodged from tree to tree to keep out of their way. Presently they calmed down and Mandy sat quietly as all the chimps clustered to gaze at her baby, but she still hurried away nervously if a large male came too close.

A new baby in a human family sometimes arouses the resentment and sometimes the delighted affection of a sibling. In chimpanzee families we see similar patterns. Little Bee was about three years old when her sister Honey Bee was born. A few times during the year that followed we saw her touch the infant, but for the most part she ignored her. At the same time she groomed her mother, Madame Bee, more than ever, as if to make up for physical contacts she no longer enjoyed, such as sleeping with her mother and riding about on her back. Because Little Bee was crippled by a clubfoot, her mother had carried her long past the normal age.

I shall never forget the mother's arrival in camp with Honey Bee. Little Bee lagged behind, limping and whimpering slightly as she struggled to keep up. She looked dazed and uncomprehending as she sat down some distance from her mother. She may or may not have realized that her sister had caused her enforced independence, but the fact remains that she seldom showed affection for her.

The relationship between Fifi and her infant brother Flint was very different. Hugo and I missed the first seven weeks of Flint's life and so never saw Fifi's initial reaction to him, but by the time we arrived she was fascinated by her tiny brother. Figan and Faben, the two older brothers, simply stared at Flint curiously and patted him occasionally. Fifi, however, continually interrupted her feeding or play to hurry over to Flo and gaze at the infant, constantly reaching out to touch him. At first Flo pushed her daughter's hand away or, if Fifi persisted, groomed her to draw her attention from Flint.

TOWARD THE END of Flint's third month, when he began crawling about over his mother's body, Fifi tried repeatedly to pull him away, but Flo always stopped her. Fifi grew increasingly frustrated, pouting, rocking to and fro, and twining her limbs into strange contortions. Yet she persevered, and when Flint was 13 weeks old we saw her take him from his mother. She clasped his foot and with cautious tugs inched Flint toward her, all the while casting sidelong glances at Flo. Suddenly, at long last, Flint lay in her arms; she held him close and kept very, very still. For a few moments Flo appeared to pay no attention to the two youngsters, but when Flint whimpered she took him back at once.

After that, Fifi took the infant more and more frequently. Sometimes she fled with Flint as though intent on kidnaping him. Then Flo would pursue the pair, making whimpering sounds herself. Eventually she permitted her daughter to carry Flint some distance away, provided she remained in sight. Fifi handled her brother gently as she groomed him or played with him, and Flo usually left them alone unless she heard Flint whimper.

At six months, Flint took his first steps. A month later he sometimes ventured as far as ten yards from his mother's side. At this age infants become very appealing to the other chimpanzees. Even irascible old J. B. reached out to pat or

Flailing her arms in possessive anger, Fifi threatens a juvenile who approaches submissively, begging to play with Flint. For months Fifi jealously guarded her infant brother.

gently tickle Flint when he wobbled near. Figan and Faben showed greater interest in their small sibling and played with him for minutes at a time.

But youngsters outside the family got little chance to play with Flint, because of Fifi's obsession. When not grooming him or playing with him, she carried him from place to place. If another youngster approached, Fifi confronted it with bristling hair, flailing her arms and stamping her feet.

As time passed, Flint developed a mind of his own and began pulling away from his sister to toddle toward some other chimp, or to make excursions on his own. He also grew bigger and heavier, and when he gripped Fifi's hair it often seemed to hurt her. Fifi's problems multiplied when the termite season began. A keen fisher, she became increasingly frustrated when Flint repeatedly grabbed her termite-laden stem, sending insects flying in all directions.

Today Flint is two and one-half years old, energetic and mischievous, and at times seems almost too much for his old mother. Fifi still plays with him a good deal, but she no longer monopolizes his day. He now spends much of his time romping with other youngsters.

Early one morning, he and Goblin were chasing about in a tree while their mothers rested on the ground nearby. I heard a cry and looked toward the infants. Flint had tired of the game and climbed down. But his playmate, almost a year younger, was stranded. He sat whimpering as he looked at a lower branch just out of his reach. Flint, hearing the cries, hurried back to his small friend and gently helped him down.

The two made the rest of the descent together, and Flint several times reached out to touch Goblin's rump as though to give encouragement.

Although chimpanzees live on a much simpler level than man, they have problems strikingly similar to some of our own. Flint's birth, for instance, not only changed Fifi's life for a while but also affected that of Gilka, another young female. In 1963, when Gilka was in her second year, her mother, Olly, often moved about with Flo and her family although, being exceptionally timid, she tended to avoid the company of other chimps. Gilka and Fifi were the best of playmates. In addition, Gilka's brother, seven-year-old Evered, was always ready for a game with his little sister.

But things changed for Gilka the following year. Evered attained adolescence and spent less time with his family, and Fifi became obsessed with Flint. Often when Gilka bounced up to her for a game, Fifi chased her away or even attacked her. And just when she had to rely more and more on her mother for companionship, Gilka also underwent the difficult weaning process.

The little chimp, formerly so gay, became increasingly lethargic. While Olly sat grooming herself or fishing for termites, Gilka "doodled" – picking twigs and plucking the leaves one by one, poking at holes in a tree trunk with her finger or a stick, or hanging from a branch for minutes on end with one foot tucked into the opposite groin.

After Gilka had behaved thus for several months she found a new playmate, a young female baboon, pale-haired and cheeky, and about the same age. We named her Goblina. When we first saw the two at play, we thought nothing of it. Young chimps and baboons frequently romp together, chasing through the trees and stopping to hit out at each other.

As the days went by, however, we realized there was something special about the relationship between Gilka and Goblina. For one thing their games differed from the usual. Not only did they chase and spar, they also rolled about on the ground together, wrestling and tickling, usually to the accompaniment of Gilka's infectious chimpanzee chuckle. Even more surprising, they did not wait until chance threw them together – they actually sought each other out!

I first saw this happen after Gilka had abruptly pulled away from a grooming by Olly and rushed up a tree. She

Ignoring her daughter for hours at a time, old and timid Olly fishes patiently for termites. Little Gilka, lonely and listless, dangles from a branch.

peered intently down the valley toward a troop of baboons some 400 yards away. Minutes later I saw a small baboon detach itself from the others and venture toward us — Goblina! Gilka saw her too and, sliding down the tree, scampered toward her new friend. When they met, she embraced Goblina and the two pressed their faces together. The gesture may have been merely a playful overture to the game that followed, but it certainly looked like a greeting between two friends.

The strange relationship lasted several months, but the two eventually drifted apart. In her fourth year, Gilka outweighed Goblina, and her rough play frightened the baboon. Then too, Gilka remained a juvenile while Goblina, at the same age, was almost full-grown; for baboons, like all monkeys, mature much faster than apes.

Before we devised our feeding scheme, my observations of the complex social structure of the chimpanzee community had been limited to the more obvious facets. My early study showed that the only group with a membership that remains constant over many months, is a mother with her younger offspring. All others at times travel alone, as well as alternating between small temporary groups and large gatherings of up to 40 individuals. I also found that small groups usually number three to six chimps, and that the large temporary gatherings occur either when the apes find some tasty food or when several males escort a sexually attractive female. At such times other females and youngsters join the group.

To investigate further proved difficult, for the chimpanzees might meet or separate anywhere within the reserve, and I could be in only one place at a time. Because of this I rarely saw the same two adults together more than once or twice in any given month. But now that the feeding area has become a permanent meeting ground, I can observe frequent interactions between the same individuals.

Thus we are learning the social status of each of the apes we know and some of the changes in status that a chimp experiences as it grows to maturity. When an infant makes brief expeditions away from its mother, it enjoys the special privileges accorded toddlers. It receives affection and almost unlimited tolerance from the others. But in time this happy state of affairs changes. During its third year the infant begins to incur mild rebuffs from its elders.

Fifi encountered her first serious threats from adults while facing another difficult trial—the drying up of her mother's milk. Once Goliath threatened her for trying to take one of his bananas. Frightened, she ran to Flo, seeking a maternal embrace and some warm milk. Flo cuddled the child, but where was the milk? Fifi, whimpering, tried each breast, but found nothing. And this happened again and again.

Bewildered and upset, Fifi went through a stage of clinging to her mother like a small infant. Flo staggered along with a daughter almost as large as she perching on her back or clinging ridiculously underneath, her coat brushing the ground. Eventually, Fifi began to adjust to her new status, learning what liberties she could take with her elders and what actions would bring a sharp reprimand.

Because her mother enjoyed a high status, Fifi had been an aggressive, defiant youngster. With females and adolescent males, she often assumed Flo's rank—acting, presumably, on the knowledge that her mother would protect her if need be. So Fifi threatened and chased chimpanzees much older than she. But at age five, when she began to leave Flo and move about for short periods with other groups, she found she had another lesson to learn: Though she could safely bully an older female while Flo stood near, the same female turned and retaliated vigorously when Fifi was alone.

On the whole, however, the juvenile leads a carefree existence. It is during adolescence that the young chimp, like the human teen-ager, goes through a difficult and frustrating period. Both sexes begin their adolescence at approximately seven years of age. When a female reaches age ten or so, she is ready to give birth. During adolescence, she not only must show great respect in interactions with adult males, but also must beware of adolescent males—even those younger than she, because they are stronger and may attack her.

T HE DAY when for the first time a female chimp becomes sexually attractive must be one of the most terrifying of her life. Males rush toward her, their hair on end. If she runs shrieking in fright they usually chase after her, enraged, or shake branches and glare at her until, still screaming, she approaches in submission.

But perhaps the young male, all things considered, leads an even more difficult life. His adolescence continues until he attains full social maturity at 12 or 13, about four years after he reaches physical maturity. In the meantime, the status of an adolescent male has been rising gradually within his family group. When Figan, at about age seven, rushed about with his hair on end, dragging branches and stamping the ground, his mother Flo paid little heed. A year later, however, Flo screamed and ran out of his path when Figan displayed in a similar way. And he dominated other females who the year before had dominated him.

But any feeling of confidence inspired in the young male as a result of his elevated position among the females is quickly dashed during interactions with mature males. Here he must learn to behave with ever-increasing caution and respect to avoid rousing aggression.

An adolescent male may watch one of his seniors enjoy food that he dares not try to share, while the tension mounts within him until he begins to rock from side to side. He may finally give vent to his frustration by leaping up, swaying branches, and dragging vegetation. Yet even this has its dangers, for often it prompts the adult males to chase and beat up the impetuous adolescent.

Figan usually avoids punishment for this kind of indiscretion. When frustrated beyond endurance in the presence of a mature male, he simply leaves the group to perform elsewhere. Beside the track leading from camp stands a tall ironwood tree with plank-buttresses, where the males often do their drumming displays when they arrive at or leave the feeding area. Whimpering softly to himself, Figan once hurried toward this tree and as he got close his crying changed to high-pitched hooting. He broke into a run, leaped onto the tree, and drummed with both feet, first on one buttress and then another. Then, his frustration apparently relieved, he returned to the group with his usual jaunty stride.

As the adolescent male grows older he becomes increasingly independent of his family group until, fully grown, he takes his place in the hierarchy of the mature males. On our return in 1966, I carefully observed Pepe and Faben to determine if their status in the community had changed. I saw that Pepe chased the lower-ranking adult males—on occasion, actually attacking poor arthritic Mr. Worzle. And Faben behaved in a similar manner.

The charging, branch-waving, and dragging displays of both were wild and impressive. From their actions it seemed obvious that they had matured and were assuming their places in the adult society. Nor would it be long, I guessed, before Pepe achieved a fairly high rank, considering his magnificent physique and the way he beat his chest like a gorilla.

There can be little doubt that this kind of charging display has a major role in the acquisition and maintenance of social status. When I became acquainted with Goliath in 1961 he dominated all the males. His charging displays were more frequent and more impressive than those of any other mature male. But at the end of 1963 Goliath lost his position to Mike, previously one of the lowliest of chimps.

Mike apparently bettered his status by developing a new kind of charging display. The change took place during our absence from the reserve. When we returned, Kris Pirozynski told us that one day Mike had seized an empty kerosene can and dragged it behind him. The can made a good deal of noise as it bounced over the uneven ground at Mike's breakneck speed. Frightened by the unusual noise, the other chimps hurried to get out of the way.

Mike learned to keep as many as three cans in front of him as he charged, batting them forward one after the other with his hands. And he would charge not once but several times. When finally he stopped, even the mighty Goliath hurried up to him. Panting nervously and bowing to the ground, he kissed, touched, or groomed him, thus acknowledging Mike's superior status.

Frantic foot-drumming of adolescent Figan resounds from the plank-buttresses of an ironwood tree. The solitary display seems to relieve tensions caused by the domination of older males.

Soon we grew to dislike Mike's noisy behavior, and we hid the cans and all other such objects he might drag. He then had to resort to mere branches and rocks like the others. But if artificial props had indeed raised his status, he no longer needed them. His position remained unchallenged. Without question, Mike is the most feared, the most respected of them all. But the status of some of the other males defies such simple classification, since it depends on which individuals are around at the time.

J. B. for example, large and aggressive in his own right, also enjoys the good fortune of being especially friendly with the great Mike. With Mike present, J. B. can dominate all the other mature males. But when Mike is absent, J. B. usually gives way to Goliath.

Then there is Mr. Worzle, bullied by all the other mature males except when he accompanies the high-ranking Leakey. On those occasions Mr. Worzle sometimes threatens, even attacks, one of his superiors. I could cite many more examples of this type of friendship in which the presence of the more powerful partner raises the status of the other.

W E HAVE NEVER SEEN similar permanent friendships of this sort between adult females, although two or more frequently gang up to threaten or chase away another. In groups consisting purely of females, or females and youngsters, there is a separate hierarchy. Until recently, Flo ruled supreme. Among the older females, however, the presence or absence of adolescent sons usually complicates the picture. Once, for instance, Flo attacked Pepe's mother, perhaps not noticing that her son was feeding nearby. Pepe responded to his mother's cries, and the two of them routed Flo.

In general, the female chimp appears more vindictive and spiteful than the male. The male loses his temper just as quickly, but after a charge or an attack he usually calms his victim with a touch or a pat and only occasionally bears a grudge. A female, on the other hand, seemingly harbors malice over a fairly long period.

Melissa, when threatened, hurries to one of the big males. Screaming in the direction of her aggressor, she stretches a hand toward her chosen champion, as though begging him to avenge her. And she sometimes does this when a high-ranking male arrives in her group ten minutes or

Attentive mother, Flo gently tickl
five-month-old Flint as he practices
new skill: dangling by one ar

more after the incident, when to all outward appearances it
has been forgotten.

Adolescent Pooch exploits a strange relationship she
enjoys with Huxley, who is probably well over 40 years old.
Pooch, only about nine now, was much younger when I first
saw the two wandering around together. There is little to
explain the strong tie between them, but many times we have
seen the old male hurry to Pooch's rescue. On one such occasion, Huxley had wandered away, leaving Pooch in camp with
Evered. We handed the youngsters their share of bananas and
a squabble broke out. Pooch uttered a small cry of fright as
Evered threatened her, and crouched in front of him submissively until he reached to pat her. They then sat side by side,
feeding peacefully as if nothing had happened.

S UDDENLY, Pooch leaped at Evered, hitting him and
screaming in rage. In our experience, it was unprece-
dented for a female to attack a male older than she, and
Evered was probably as surprised as we were. Then we saw
Huxley hurrying down the slope, presumably in response to
Pooch's first cry. Hair on end, the old male stood looking at
the wrangling youngsters, then charged toward them.

After a short scuffle, Huxley walked away, his hair
sinking to its normal position. Pooch watched calmly as Evered
screamed in rage until his throat cramped. Before following
her protector, Pooch walked up to Evered and made a face I
have never seen before or since. It could best be described
as a smirk.

How can we account for the attachment between Huxley and Pooch? Huxley is far too old to be her brother, nor
can we suppose him to be her father: Because of the promiscu-
ity of the chimp no male could ever know his own offspring.

We do wonder, however, if some of the other friendships may be founded on family relationships. Are Leakey
and Mr. Worzle brothers? Certainly they have a similar muta-
tion of the eyes. Mr. Worzle, as I have mentioned, has eyes
that resemble those of a man. To a lesser extent, Leakey shares
this startling feature. He has enough white in his eyes to give
him something of Mr. Worzle's appearance.

Perhaps the companionship between young siblings
develops into the casual but persistent friendships that we see
between some of the adult chimpanzees.

Like a human child, an infant chimp can spend as much time playing with food as eating it. Flint, aged two, picks a *Protea* blossom, stem and all. Instead of munching it as an adult would, he pokes a finger into the center. But drowsiness catches up with him while he tears the flower apart. Finally, almost asleep, he sucks idly on the petals.

Reaching up lazily, Flo caresses Flint,
who swings on a palm frond as his mother rests. She sits, trusting but watchful,

while Jane pets Fifi and Flint. At first, Flo held baby Flint securely whenever his five-year-old sister touched him (lower left); later she allowed the youngsters to play together. Below, Flint reaches back to grab for Fifi's ears.

Two heedless mothers—and an alert one. Marina ignores Merlin, who looks a bit bored (upper left). Melissa lets three-month-old Goblin struggle vainly to reach her lap, disregarding his whimpers for the moment (right). Flint stands on Flo's back before settling himself to ride jockey-style. Flo guards him from every danger—including Jane's foam-rubber mattress. When Fifi (far left) carried Flint to play on it, Flo promptly took him away, glancing about uneasily.

Mischievous Fifi settles down on a log in the relaxed position chimps often take, forearms on knees, hands dangling, feet apart. Above, she perches on a tent guy rope. To eat a banana in peace, she sometimes climbs the rope instead of going up a tree like other young chimps.

My toy! Flint balances a *Strychnos* fruit on his shoulder. About the size of a tennis ball, it rolls smoothly when kicked, and the tough rind makes it durable. Jane has never seen one youngster roll the fruit to another, but she reports a "keep-away" game —one attempts to steal the ball while the other tries to save it for himself.

Teetering on a dead branch, two-year-old Merlin balances until the twig
gives way and he jumps to the ground a few feet below. With Flo nearby,
five-month-old Flint practices climbing on two slender saplings. Keeping
a tight grip with one foot and one hand, he puts his left thumb in his
mouth. Flo swings easily from a stout branch as he clutches her foot.
Jane comments: "His expression's a play face, all excitement — perhaps
Flo's tickling him with her toes."

*Baby Flint bungles an early attempt
to build a play nest. He begins correctly
by bending down grass but then, instead
of sitting on the stems as he should,
he pushes them firmly into his lap.*

7

Only the Beginning

"SURELY there can't be much more to find out about those chimps of yours," one visitor remarked as he watched Flo and her family wander away from the observation area and disappear into the forest. Hugo and I smiled to ourselves. We have grown used to explaining that many of the most important and fascinating questions can be answered only if we keep up our records for the next ten to twenty years.

How long, for example, do chimpanzee family relationships endure? When fully grown, will Fifi and her brothers spend more time together than with other chimps? What effect will Flo's changing status have on her offspring? She was much younger when she gave birth to Faben, and probably less dominant than when Flint was born. What social ranks will the brothers hold as a consequence? How long will Mike remain the dominant male? And if he loses his status while still in his prime, what factors will be at work?

By persevering at the reserve we hope to find the answers to these questions and to many more. Such matters interest not only us, but also students of human behavior — anthropologists, psychologists, and sociologists. For if, as Hugo and I firmly believe, many of the fundamental behavior patterns of man and ape share a common origin in the distant past, then a thorough knowledge of ape behavior may well prove invaluable to a better understanding of man's behavior. Chimpanzees in the wild make good subjects for the kind of study we are pursuing because they possess a range of emotions similar to man's and demonstrate a certain capacity for reasoned thinking.

Moreover, chimpanzee society imposes fewer inhibitions than any society of humans living today. Even in the chimpanzee community, of course, some laws of conduct exist, as in any animal group: for instance, an older animal will not normally attack an infant. But the chimps' society is freer than ours, so it is easier to see the reasons for a chimp's action than to understand a similar action performed by a man.

Let me relate, as an example, the pitiable experiences of the orphan, Merlin. His story may give clues as to the extent to which childhood experiences affect a human adult.

In May, 1965, while Hugo and I were in England, Merlin and his ailing mother stopped visiting camp. Days passed, until our assistants at the reserve gave up hope of ever seeing Merlin again. Ten weeks had gone by when he arrived at the camp with his big brother Pepe. When Hugo and I returned to the reserve, Edna Koning told us the full story.

When Merlin so unexpectedly reappeared after his long absence, the chimpanzees in the camp rushed to greet him, embracing, kissing, and grooming him. It seemed obvious that they too had not seen him for some time. Finally he curled up, as though very tired, beside Pepe.

"The thing that struck us," Edna said, "was the strained, sad look on his face. His eyes seemed huge and glazed. But he appeared healthy apart from a tight, hard tummy."

Later that morning his sister Miff arrived. She rushed to her small brother and at that moment, to all intents and purposes, adopted him. She let him sleep beside her at night, protected him as best she could, and waited for him when she moved from place to place.

What happened to him during those two and a half months? We can only guess. Perhaps his mother became too weak to walk farther, made herself a large nest, and died there with Merlin close by. We can only imagine how the orphan must have pressed himself against her cold body, seeking warmth, trying to suckle from her breasts. Many times he must have pulled her hand toward him, trying to make her groom him or play with him. How bewildered and anxious he must have become—how cold and hungry! Then perhaps Pepe passed nearby, and Merlin finally left the corpse of his mother to follow his older brother.

For several months after his return Merlin behaved like a normal youngster. But Miff, though tolerant and protective toward him, could not compensate for the loss of his mother. And Pepe, though he roamed with his family more

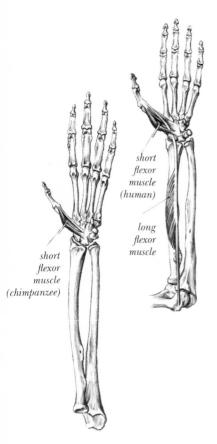

Bone structure of the human hand and that of the chimpanzee reveals an all-important difference: Man's longer thumb can meet the tip of the forefinger in a precision grip no other animal can duplicate.

short flexor muscle (human)

long flexor muscle

short flexor muscle (chimpanzee)

frequently than he had during the previous year, was not with Merlin enough to provide him a real source of protection.

Hugo and I found that Merlin was no longer the gay, mischievous youngster we remembered. Today, at three, he is not only stunted in growth and physically unfit, but also appears neurotic. For hours he sits rocking gently from side to side. Grooming himself with the concentration of an adult, he often pulls out his hairs and nibbles at the roots—as chimpanzees in captivity sometimes do.

Rather than approach other youngsters for a game, Merlin goes to the adults for grooming. Sometimes Flint tries to play with him, but Merlin merely crouches to the ground and if Flint persists often turns and attacks him. Occasionally he plays with an infant, but not in the carefree fashion of a normal three-year-old. Instead, he reaches out a hand and idly tickles the little one, reminding us of an indulgent adult.

Merlin has, in fact, suffered a shattering loss. Will all traces of his seeming neurosis finally disappear, or will he always behave as he does today? Will he be a low-ranking male, dominated by others all his life? Or will he become bad-tempered and aggressive, as if to avenge his unhappy childhood? Only long observation can tell us.

The actions of the human adult may reveal comparatively little about the influence of his early experiences, for man exercises sufficient self-control in most cases to present a normal exterior. A chimpanzee, however, possesses no such self-control. Therefore, if Merlin lives to maturity, any marks left by his early deprivation should show clearly in his behavior. Whatever the outcome, his story may help to clarify much-debated problems of bringing up human children.

Yes, we can still learn much from the chimpanzee in the wild, much that may benefit mankind. In addition, because of his humanlike qualities, this ape is of inestimable value to many branches of scientific research. His ability to solve simple problems has helped the psychologist to understand the learning process. As a part of the United States' space program, doctors have used chimpanzees in test flights and in ground studies to determine the effects of space travel on astronauts.

Thus it is tragic that the chimpanzee—so interesting in himself, so valuable to man—is rapidly being exterminated in his native Africa. It is horrifying to realize that each

Long, muscular fingers fit the chimpanzee for walking on all fours or for swinging through trees. Powerful hands and arms easily carry a 175-pound male among the branches.

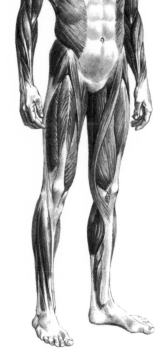

chimpanzee killed had, like tough old Flo or gentle David Greybeard, his own highly individual temperament and character. In some parts of Africa chimps are hunted for food. We hear of chimpanzee mothers cut up and sold for meat, and their infants carried away for sale. In other places the chimps may die of starvation as the advance of agriculture and settlement destroys their forest homes.

Many governments in Africa, especially those of Tanzania and Kenya, take active and enlightened steps to protect areas where wild animals can survive the onslaught of civilization. Our work at the Gombe Stream would be impossible without the understanding and cooperation of the Tanzanian government.

And the World Wildlife Fund has opened a special Chimpanzee Account for contributions to help establish a series of chimpanzee sanctuaries in Africa.* To Hugo and me, and to our assistants at the reserve, the hope that at least some

*World Wildlife Fund: 910 17th Street, N.W., Washington, D. C. 20006, or 2 Caxton Street, Westminster, London, S.W. 1.

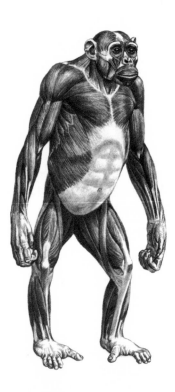

Exposed muscles show the similarities and differences of man and ape. A chimpanzee cannot fully straighten his thighs and lock his knees as man does, but the ape's long arms and proportionately shorter legs equip him for life among the trees.

chimp populations may be saved in this way, is most comforting. We know, only too well, the helpless suffering of injured chimpanzees in the wild. Fortunately, we see few bad wounds in the reserve, where the chimp finds protection from his greatest enemy—man.

The chimps tolerate and, to a great extent, trust us, but none of them would let us handle them to administer medical aid. If we tried, the patient would undoubtedly turn and bite. Also, he would scream in fright or threat. This would probably cause any adult male present to attack us—the others to lose their faith in us. These chimpanzees are, after all, wild animals. So we could only watch and sympathize when Mandy came into camp with her mutilated infant, when David Greybeard arrived in camp with a sprained leg, when Merlin sat shivering with cold during the heavy rains.

On happy occasions, too, we long to touch our chimpanzee subjects. For a time we actually did allow some of the youngsters—Figan, Fifi, Flint—to play with us. But we soon had to discourage this. Ultimately it would have affected their

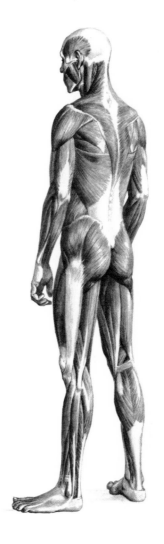

natural behavior. Moreover, when they grow up they will be much stronger than we. If they realized this, they might well turn and attack us, as they would attack a weaker chimp during one of those sudden fits of anger characteristic of all chimpanzees. Indeed, when some of the adult males charge in their wild displays, our safety probably depends on the fact that they respect us. Our upright stance seems to make them feel that we are the stronger.

Yet, even though we must remain spectators, we cannot help but become emotionally involved in the doings of the various chimps in the Gombe Stream community. Each one has such a distinct personality. Only a short time ago Hugo and I sat with a small group of chimpanzees. We had followed them away from camp into the cool forest on the far side of the valley. We heard only the rushing stream, the shrilling of cicadas, and the occasional trill or chirp of a forest bird. Nearby, David and Goliath idly groomed each other, their eyes half closed with drowsiness.

Young Flint sat in a clump of grass, expertly bending the stems and sitting on them to build a play nest. As I watched, I thought back to an earlier effort when he was just six months old. He had managed to bend one small plant and hold it against the ground with his leg, but then, after pulling down several blades of grass, he apparently became confused—he pushed them firmly into his lap instead of sitting on them! The practice infants get in such play may enable them later to construct strong, comfortable beds.

Fifi, our wicked Fifi, lay stretched on the ground with her eyes fast shut and her expression angelic. Who could tell, unless they knew her as we do, that behind that mask of innocence lurks one of the most mischievous of chimpanzees? Fifi, with her expressive face, her frustration and disappointment when she was not allowed to fondle baby Flint, stole the hearts of the thousands of people who saw the lecture film Hugo edited for the National Geographic Society.

Adolescent Figan sat grooming his mother, old Flo. One of our cleverest chimps, he had quickly learned how to release the levers that open the banana boxes. Often he seems deliberately to lead the big males out of camp, only to return alone some ten minutes later and eat his fill of bananas without danger of being chased by the older males. His very cleverness has made him one of our favorites. As he carefully groomed

Designed for climbing, the long, flexible great toe of the chimpanzee gives his foot an ability to grip not possessed by man. For the ape, the feet function as a second pair of hands, with toes coordinating almost as well as fingers.

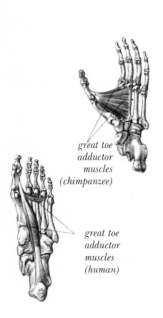

great toe
adductor
muscles
(chimpanzee)

great toe
adductor
muscles
(human)

his mother, she stared absently into space. "She looks like an old, old woman, dreaming of her past," Hugo remarked.

With her ugly face and her flat, worn teeth, Flo is indeed an old, old female. She looks frail and rather tired. For the most part she simply sits or lies about while the events of the chimpanzee world swirl and eddy around her. Too often, though, she gets involved in a fight, for she no longer seems to have the wits to keep out of the way. When Flint screams in fright, his sister Fifi often hurries to his rescue while his mother just stands watching.

On rare occasions, she charges and stamps after the other females with something of her old spirit, but such assertions of authority seem fast drawing to an end. As though they sense Flo's declining power, the other females one by one are beginning to usurp her hard-won status.

As I sat quietly, I heard the whir of Hugo's camera. Flint, tickled beyond endurance by Faben, had run to seek refuge behind Flo. Hugo filmed the two as they chased round and round their mother. Figan and Fifi followed suit, unable to resist one of their favorite games. Buffeted by her children, Flo grabbed out at their feet, as though trying to trip them up. Not too long ago, she would have joined in herself and the whole family might have chased round and round a tree. Now she seems quite content to play a less active part. Soon the game ended. Flint flung himself into his mother's arms for a drink of milk, and the others lay down to rest.

"Won't it be exciting when Fifi has her first baby?" Hugo asked, as he put aside his camera. "I do hope the research will still be going on, and that I shall be able to film it."

"Yes," I replied, "I certainly hope so too. I was just thinking about the future as well — thinking how sad it will be when Flo dies, though I should think Flint will be able to fend for himself by the time that happens."

I T WILL BE a sad day too when my first chimpanzee acquaintance, David Greybeard, is no more. To me, he is not just a chimpanzee — he is, quite truly, a friend.

My close contact with him led to the establishment of a bond between man and ape, a bond based on mutual trust and respect — in a sense, a friendship. Of course I must always play the part of the observer, who does not interfere, and I must never forget that I am studying the natural behavior of wild

creatures. They remind me of this duty themselves. They do not imitate human gestures and behavior, as captive chimps will do. When they see me after a long separation, they give no display of affection, as would a pet. They merely show recognition by ignoring me completely. If I were a stranger, they would run away or hide. To these chimpanzees man is a distinct creature, normally to be avoided, but in certain special cases to be tolerated. This is what I mean, generally, by "friendship" with the chimps.

WITH DAVID IT IS DIFFERENT. As I sat there that hot afternoon, I gazed at him. He had stopped grooming Goliath and was stretched out asleep. It is David, alone of all the chimps, who has reached out to me across the barriers of species and language that separate ape from man. And he acted of his own free will. I thought back to that incident. I was alone with David that day, deep in the forest. I held out a palm nut to him and, although he did not want it, he accepted my offering. For a full ten seconds, he held my hand gently and firmly in his. Finally, with a last glance at the nut, he let it fall to the ground.

In that brief, exalted moment I had felt a thrill of communication with a wild chimpanzee — not by a scientific interpretation of his behavior, but rather by an instinctive understanding of his gesture. He had reached out to reassure me by the pressure of his fingers. Although he rejected my gift, he gave me one of his own: a primitive communion based on touch, so distinct from the sophisticated communion based on intellect.

I turned to Hugo. "Doesn't it seem strange," I said, "that on the emotional level chimps are so nearly human, yet culturally and intellectually we are so widely separated?"

"Yes," Hugo replied, "but chimps aren't really animals, and they aren't men, of course. Just strange and very wonderful in-between creatures."

We gazed at David Greybeard and Goliath, at Flo and her family, resting so peacefully, so blissfully unaware of their own mystery, of the challenge their mere existence hurls at the scientist, at the philosopher. At that moment David awakened. As we contemplated this marvelous creature, he sat up and grunted. It was time to climb into the branches overhead for another stomachful of figs.

Determining the chimpanzees' diet, Jane, with assistant Edna Koning, sifts, sorts, and classifies remains of plants and animals in the apes' dung. Among recent finds: two small teeth and a tiny hoof from young bushbuck.

Hugo extends a microphone and adjusts the volume on his tape recorder to capture a chimp's panting laughter.

Joining Figan and Jane for lunch, members of the Research Committee observe the progress of her work. From left: Dr. Leonard Carmichael, Chairman of the Committee and a Vice President of the National Geographic Society, Dr. Melvin M. Payne, the Society's Executive Vice President, and Dr. T. Dale Stewart of the Smithsonian Institution.

Jane and her mother wrap and seal a chimpanzee skeleton in plastic to preserve it for further study. Dominic had found the body floating in a stream. Color-coded chart (below) helps in keeping daily behavioral records on all the chimps that appear at the camp.

Separated from her mother, Fifi whimpers.
Figan, bobbing submissively, pants a greeting.

Mike grimaces with fear.
Lips compressed, Rodolf shows annoyance.

Relaxed Figan yawns sleepily.

From sleepy yawn to excited hoot, the chimpanzees' highly mobile faces reflect their many moods and emotions. Facial muscles and bone structure similar to man's permit a wide range of startlingly familiar expressions — a quality that adds to Jane's difficulties in studying objectively these "all-too-human animals." Lips curved as in a smile, however, may express irritation, and when crying or whimpering, chimpanzees shed no tears.

Mike glares before beginning a charging display.
Cradling two-day-old Goblin, Melissa hoots.

ust making a face, Goliath curls his flexible lip.
epe's expression mingles excitement and fear.

'orzle's white eyes give him a sinister appearance.

Figan's look of rage is only a frustration yawn.

Pathetic Merlin—orphaned and sickly—huddles in the rain, and Flo and her exuberant family call with excitement. In future work, Jane hopes to learn more about these highly individual animals. She will observe Merlin to find if he ever truly recovers from the shattering loss of his mother and his early hardships. Flo's offspring warrant further study as well, for as their mother grows older and declines in rank, their relationships with each other and with other chimps will certainly change. As Jane points out: "... many of the most important and fascinating questions can be answered only if we keep up our records for the next ten to twenty years."

Content in their treetop perches, at ease with their human observers, the mysterious, captivating chimps survey their remote African home.

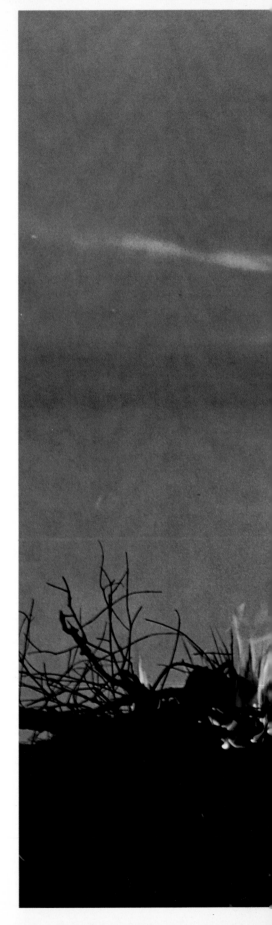

IN THE FAINT LIGHT of evening, Jane makes a last entry in her notebook as she prepares to remain overnight in the mountains near a group of sleeping chimpanzees. At dawn, when the apes awaken, she will begin another day of observation. Determination and courage, and a consuming love of animals, brought her to the Gombe Stream Game Reserve in 1960, and years filled with hard work, excitement, and danger, have won her the success she sought. The frustration of the early months, when the chimps fled at the sight of her, turned to exhilaration when she finally gained their acceptance and trust and was able to live and work among them. She saw them making and using simple tools, killing and eating small animals, and living undisturbed within their own community. Her reports interest anthropologists, psychologists, and sociologists — all the students of human behavior — for the wild ape may in some ways resemble man's forebears. Today, the work at the reserve goes on. There are new goals to reach, new chimps to study. Jane is not really alone with her campfire and her notebook — she is alone with her remarkable friends, the wild chimpanzees.

Index

Bibliography

The reader may wish to refer to the following books about the behavior of chimpanzees and other primates:

Köhler, W., *The Mentality of Apes*, New York, Harcourt Brace, 1925. An interesting report of a pioneer study of chimpanzees, with special reference to their insight in the solution of problems.

Yerkes, R. M., and Yerkes, A. W., *The Great Apes: A Study of Anthropoid Life*, New Haven, Yale University Press, 1929 (fourth printing, 1953). A fine summary of research up to 1929, with a wise evaluation of the scientific significance of this field of study.

Yerkes, R. M., *Chimpanzees: A Laboratory Colony*, New Haven, Yale University Press, 1943. An excellent report of the varied and important work of the Yale Laboratories (later named the Yerkes Laboratories) of Primate Biology at Orange Park, Florida.

Carpenter, C. R., *Naturalistic Behavior of Nonhuman Primates*, University Park, Pennsylvania State University Press, 1964. A republication of original monographs and articles which have become basic in primatology.

DeVore, I. (Editor), *Primate Behavior: Field Studies of Monkeys and Apes*, New York, Holt, Rinehart and Winston, 1965. Each chapter is by a well-known modern authority. Those by Jane Goodall and by Vernon and Francis Reynolds deal with wild chimpanzees and present technical scientific information of great value. This book has an excellent bibliography.

Schrier, A. M., Harlow, H. F., Stollnitz, F. (Editors), *Behavior of Nonhuman Primates: Modern Research Trends* (2 vols.), New York, Academic Press, 1965. In 15 chapters, recognized authorities summarize the current state of research in specialized fields such as habit formation, social behavior, perception, and age changes in behavior during individual development.

Reynolds, Vernon, *Budongo, an African Forest and its Chimpanzees*, Garden City, Natural History Press, 1965. An account of an eight months' field study of wild chimpanzees in Uganda.

COMPOSITION BY NATIONAL GEOGRAPHIC'S PHOTOTYPOGRAPHIC DIVISION, HERMAN J. A. C. ARENS, DIRECTOR; JOHN E. McCONNELL, MANAGER. PRINTED AND BOUND BY FAWCETT-HAYNES PRINTING CORPORATION, ROCKVILLE, MARYLAND. COLOR SEPARATIONS BY LANMAN ENGRAVING COMPANY, ALEXANDRIA, VIRGINIA; BECK ENGRAVING COMPANY, PHILADELPHIA, PENNSYLVANIA; AND GRAPHIC COLOR PLATE, INC., STAMFORD, CONNECTICUT.